SUPERSIZE 'EM!
22 quilts from oversized blocks

Debby Kratovil

MISSION STATEMENT

Dedicated to providing quality products and
service to inspire creativity.

CREDITS

President & CEO • Tom Wierzbicki

Editor-in-Chief • Mary V. Green

Managing Editor • Tina Cook

Developmental Editor • Karen Costello Soltys

Technical Editor • Laurie Baker

Copy Editor • Liz McGehee

Design Director • Stan Green

Production Manager • Regina Girard

Illustrator • Adrienne Smitke

Cover & Text Designer • Shelly Garrison

Photographer • Brent Kane

Supersize 'Em! 22 Quilts from Oversized Blocks
© 2009 by Debby Kratovil

That Patchwork Place® is an imprint of
Martingale & Company®.

Martingale & Company
20205 144th Ave. NE
Woodinville, WA 98072-8478 USA
www.martingale-pub.com

Printed in China
14 13 12 11 10 09   8 7 6 5 4 3 2 1

Library of Congress Cataloging-in-Publication Data
Library of Congress Control Number: 2008050000

ISBN: 978-1-56477-873-4

DEDICATION

This book would not be possible without the love and support of my husband, Phil, and my three lovely daughters, Audrey, Hilary, and Valery. They understand my passion for creating quilts from fabric that, most of the time, is strewn all over the sewing-room floor. They have a healthy respect for my deadlines because this livelihood has paid the mortgage and college bills. But most of all, I recognize that my creative ways have flowed from the Great Designer, who never fails to surprise me with all the beauty this world has to offer for inspiration. My business name, Quilter by Design, is a tribute to Him.

ACKNOWLEDGMENTS

It was my association with Sarah Phillips, owner of Intown Quilters in the Atlanta, Georgia, metro area, that gave me the nudge to work with big-print fabrics. Sarah is a savvy shop owner who knows that her customers like to make big quilts, and that sells a lot of fabric! She likes a lot of shop samples to inspire her clientele. Many times, she would place a bundle of eye-popping fabrics in my hands and say, "Go sew!" I would run home and get a quilt top done in a few days and create a class from it. Good samples make good classes and sell good fabrics.

I could not make beautiful quilts without beautiful fabrics. Being a professional in the quilting industry for more than 15 years has put me in contact with the companies that make glorious fabric. I have sewn for the best, but in particular I am indebted to the following companies for their generous supplies: Blank Textiles, Windham Fabrics, and Westminster Fabrics. They trusted my judgment when it came to design and execution. I have been honored to see my quilts grace more than two dozen magazine covers. This could not happen with ugly fabric! Thank you, fabric companies, for keeping me in stitches.

CONTENTS

INTRODUCTION • 6

SPECIAL TECHNIQUES • 7

ABOUT THE AUTHOR • 111

Dancing with the Flowers • 12

Princess Feather • 16

Glorious Blooms • 20

Jeweled Crazy Hearts • 24

Snow Crystals • 28

Diamond Head • 32

Peacock Garden • 36

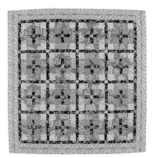

Asian Allegory • 40

The Comfort Quilt • 44

Good-Luck Pansies • 48

Texas Stars • 52

It's Easy Being Green • 58

Facets of Color Quilt • 62

Facets of Color Table Runner • 68

That Spikey Thing • 72

Secret Garden Album • 76

Modern Grace • 80

Starry, Starry Brights • 84

Trick-or-Treat Mice • 88

Diadem • 92

Carriage Crossing • 98

Cloisonné Diamonds • 104

INTRODUCTION

Big blocks are a great way to finish a quilt in less time. The pieces in each block are larger, which makes it go together quicker and easier, and just a few blocks make a good-sized wall hanging. Add sashing and borders, and you've got a bed-sized quilt in no time. Some may think it's just a lazy way to get a quilt finished, but who can argue with being able to accomplish more in less time?

While saving time is a great advantage, perhaps an even bigger asset to making big blocks is that the larger pieces are a great way to showcase big, bold prints that you don't want to cut up into itsy-bitsy pieces. With inspiration from the projects in this book, you can pull out your large-scale prints and slice into them without fear!

I love using big, bold, color-drenched fabrics. They create quilts that are full of spunk and that catch the eye. I've been making quilts for magazines for years, and the editors and publishers taught me early on that quilts made from low-contrast fabrics don't photograph well. More excitement is created by using high-contrast fabrics, and they also make it easier for the reader to see where one fabric ends and another begins. I've been mixing prints and colors with great abandon ever since and have had more than 25 quilts on the covers of quilting magazines.

Many quilters feel that they must use the same fabrics as the designer to have successful results. Unfortunately, fabric lines don't stick around long, and unless you already own a fabric you've seen in one of the quilts in this book, the chances of finding it are somewhat slim. My guess is that you probably have a large-scale print or two lying around waiting for just the right project. Pull them out and browse through the 22 projects in this book. One of them is bound to work. Then, look through your stash for companion fabrics, and if you have none, go shopping! Pick fabrics you love, and you can't go wrong.

Are there any rules to working with big blocks and big prints? Not really. One thing that I do recommend is to abandon fussy cutting. Occasionally, it's fun to highlight a specific motif, as in the block centers of "Carriage Crossing" (page 98), but for the most part, just cut the fabric, even if a huge flower is dissected. "Surprise cutting," as I like to call it, is whimsical, free form, and fun. Other than that, follow the same guidelines as you would when making any other type of quilt: make sure your ¼" seam allowances are as perfect as possible; measure twice, cut once; cut and sew a sample block before cutting out the pieces for an entire quilt; and don't be afraid to ask for advice if you get stuck. And remember, it's not a race, it's a hobby—have fun!

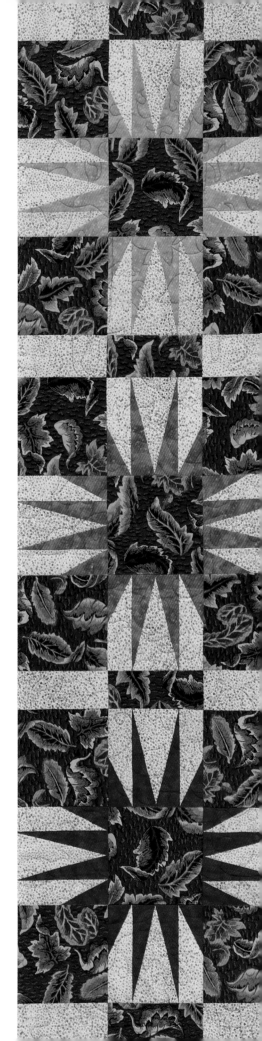

Special TECHNIQUES

There are a lot of books that cover the basics of making a quilt, so I'm not going to take up a lot of space repeating what you probably already know—I'd rather give you more quilt designs! However, I did feel that it was necessary to include instructions for paper piecing, which is used for five of the quilts in this book, and for techniques that I have my own way of doing, such as mitering corners and binding the quilt edges. Instructions for these techniques can be found on the pages that follow.

PAPER PIECING

Paper piecing is an easy way to achieve accurate points and to piece complex designs. Like any technique, there are several ways to paper piece, and there are lots of tools on the market to make it easier. I've listed some of those below.

Through trial and error, I've found that the method given here works the best for me. If you've never paper pieced before, be aware that the pattern is the reverse image of the finished block. In order to achieve the mirror image of the pattern, you will be placing the fabric on the unmarked side of the pattern and sewing from the marked side.

Tools and Supplies

6" and 12" Add-A-Quarter rulers: These rulers are invaluable for trimming the seam allowances *before* adding the next patch. They take the guesswork out of fabric placement and keep you from having to hold the pattern and fabric up to a light source to see what's going on.

Foundation paper: My favorite paper is newsprint because it is thin, easy to tear away, and cheap! Check your local grocery store or big box store for tablets created for children's scribble pads. Tracing paper is also an excellent choice. Avoid computer paper; it's too heavy and will put a strain on your stitches when you tear it away.

Open-toe presser foot: This foot allows you to see the sewing line better.

Postcard or other lightweight card stock: A 4" x 6" postcard or 3" x 5" index card placed on the sewing line ensures a clean, neat fold when the pattern is turned back to trim the seam allowance.

Size 90/14 sewing-machine needles: The larger size perforates the foundation paper and makes paper removal easier.

Making the Foundations

1. Rule No. 1 of foundation piecing is *never* sew on your master pattern, so you'll need to make copies of the patterns provided in the book using one of the following methods. Make as many copies as required for the design you are working on, plus one extra for reference. Some blocks are made from a single unit and others are assembled from multiple units, so you will need to make copies of all the required patterns. The patterns will be cut apart later, so you can copy as many as will fit on each piece of paper.

   - Use a photocopier. If you select this method, make one copy first, and then compare it to the master copy. Distortion can occur with some photocopy machines.

   - Trace each copy by hand. This is very labor intensive, but if it is your only option, use a light box or a well-lit window to aid you in the process, and use a ruler to help you make straight, accurate lines. Be sure to transfer the number and fabric for each section onto each pattern.

   - Needle punch multiple foundations using an unthreaded sewing machine. See "Needle-Punched Foundations" on page 8 for specifics.

2. Cut the patterns apart if there is more than one on a page. Don't leave any more than ½" of extra paper around the outside lines of each pattern.

3. To make sure you stitch the fabrics in the correct areas, tape or glue a piece of the appropriate fabric to each section on the extra pattern you made. Keep this near your sewing machine as a reference. Remember, the paper pattern is the reverse or mirror image of the finished unit or block.

Needle-Punched Foundations

If you can't get to the photocopy store to make multiples of your foundation patterns, don't worry. You have everything you need at home if you have a sewing machine, a stapler, and foundation paper. This method even improves the tedious task of removing the paper from your finished blocks because each line gets stitched twice!

1. Trace the master pattern onto a piece of paper.

2. Layer no more than six pieces of foundation paper on top of each other. The paper should be at least the same size or larger than the copied pattern. Place the copy of the pattern on the top of the stack. Staple the layers together in two or three places, well away from the stitching lines.

3. Remove the thread from your sewing machine's needle and bobbin. Machine stitch along every line of your foundation pattern, including the outside edges marking the ¼" seam allowance. This method of punching holes in the stack of papers is actually transferring the lines to each paper in the stack! Neat, huh?

4. Remove the staples, but keep the stack together. Take the copied pattern from the top of the stack. Now, remove one paper at a time, carefully transferring the numbers from the copied pattern to the correct positions of each needle-punched pattern. If a pattern is symmetrical (as in "Diadem," "Facets of Color," and "That Spikey Thing") you can't really mix up the placement of the patches, but if you are working on "Snow Crystals," you must take care to transfer the numbers exactly as they appear on your photocopy on the top of the stack.

5. Trim away any excess paper from the patterns so there is no more than ½" of paper extending beyond the outer needle-punched lines.

Cutting the Fabric Pieces

I like to cut the fabrics for each numbered area on the pattern to an approximate size before I begin paper piecing. I've indicated the size to cut your pieces for all the projects in this book so you don't have to worry about that here, but if you venture out into other paper-pieced patterns, to estimate the size to cut the piece to cover a specific area, I measure the area at the widest spot and then cut a piece at least 1" wider and longer than the shape. Often I will work with a strip of fabric cut to the width determined, and then just cut off the excess strip once the area is covered. Many of the areas on the patterns you'll find in this book are triangular and the pieces can be cut from a square that has been cut in half diagonally. For pieces like that, I generally add a generous 1½" to the measurement.

Sewing the Pieces in Place

1. Place the pattern on your work surface so the unprinted side is face up. Pick up the fabric piece for section 1 and place the wrong side of the fabric on the pattern so that it covers section 1 by at least ¼" on all sides. Lightly glue using a glue stick (you just need a dab of glue to keep the fabric from shifting) or pin the fabric in place.

2. Turn the pattern over so the printed side is face up. Place the postcard or index card along the line between sections 1 and 2. Fold the pattern back on this line and over the card. Trim the fabric that extends beyond the fold to ¼". If you are using the Add-A-Quarter ruler, place the lip of the ruler snugly against the fold and trim the fabric. You now have an edge that's cut at exactly the right angle to place the piece for section 2.

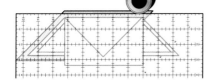

3 Turn the pattern over to the unmarked side. With right sides together, place the fabric piece for section 2 over fabric 1, aligning the trimmed edge of piece 1 with the appropriate raw edge of piece 2. Carefully flip the section 2 fabric over to make sure it covers section 2, with at least ¼" extra along all the sides. Flip the section 2 fabric back into place, and pin the pieces together, taking care to keep the pin well away from the sewing line.

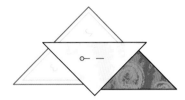

4 Turn the pattern over to the marked side. Using a size 90/14 sewing-machine needle and a stitch length of 15 to 20 stitches per inch, stitch on the line between sections 1 and 2, beginning and ending off the edge of the pattern. This shorter stitch length creates more perforations and makes it easier to tear away the paper foundation later. Remove the pin.

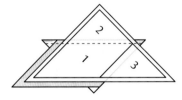

5 Flip the pattern over to the unmarked side and finger-press the fabric piece in place over section 2. Make sure section 2 is completely covered and there is at least ¼" extra on the unstitched sides.

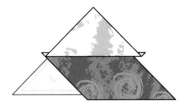

6 Now, turn the pattern over to the printed side and lay the postcard or index card on the line between sections 1 and 3. Fold the pattern back and trim the section 1 fabric to ¼". Add the section 3 fabric in the same manner as you did for section 2.

7 Continue adding the fabric pieces in this manner, working in numerical order. Once all of the pieces have been added, press the unit or block from the fabric side with an iron. Don't press on the paper side, especially if you've printed your patterns with an inkjet printer or used a photocopy machine; the ink and laser toner will transfer to your iron and then onto your fabric.

8 Use a rotary ruler and cutter to trim any excess fabric extending beyond the outer edges of the unit or block.

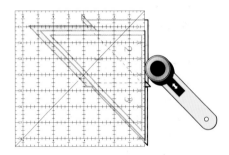

Removing the Papers

Don't remove the paper from the units or blocks until you are finished paper piecing all of the required pieces for the project. Some paper piecers choose to leave their papers on until they are finished sewing the quilt, but I don't like to remove the paper from the seam allowances so I remove it right before I join the units or blocks. Don't agonize over removing every little bit of paper. Remember, it's nonwoven pulp and will wash out if the quilt is laundered.

To remove the foundations, support the stitched edge of the seam with your thumb and gently tug on the paper with the thumb and forefinger of your other hand. If the paper is especially stubborn, spritz it with water, let sit for a minute or two, and then remove it with your fingers or tweezers.

Joining Units

Some blocks require stitching more than one unit together to complete the block. Refer to the project instructions for specifics on sewing the units together, matching seams as you would any other project. Press the seam allowances open to reduce bulk.

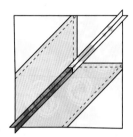

MAGICAL MITERED CORNERS

For those times when your border fabric cries out for a mitered corner—when using plaid or striped fabric, for example—consider using this method, which bypasses the traditional set-in seam and guarantees a perfect join with almost invisible stitching.

1. Determine the border width.

2. Measure the length and width of your quilt top. It is best to take these measurements through the center of the quilt. Add twice the width of the border plus 1" or 2" additional to each of these measurements, and then cut two strips to this length and the width determined in step 1.

3. Center and pin the side border strips to the sides of the quilt top, right sides together. Sew the border in place from one edge of the quilt top to the opposite edge. There is no need to start and stop at the 1/4" point as you do with most mitering techniques. Press the seam allowances toward the quilt top.

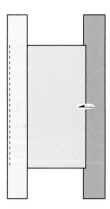

4. Center and pin the top and bottom borders to the quilt top. Insert the needle into the seam of the side border (which should be 1/4" from the quilt-top edge), and sew until you reach the seam of the opposite side border; backstitch. Press the seam allowance away from the quilt top.

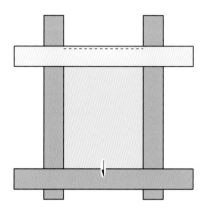

5. Fold under the ends of the top and bottom border strips so they form a 45° angle (miter) at each corner; press well. Pin down the angled edge and blindstitch it in place by machine or hand. If you choose to machine stitch, monofilament thread is a good choice for this task. Trim away the excess fabric from the four corners on the wrong side of the quilt, leaving a 1/4" seam allowance. Press well.

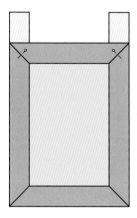

MACHINE-STITCHED BINDING

I use a binding method that is not very traditional, but it is quick, it works, and it gives me more time to make more quilts! The big difference in my method is that the binding is sewn on from the back, and then brought to the front and topstitched in place by machine. I also prefer to cut my binding strips 2 1/8" to 2 1/4" wide, which is a little wider than normal. This allows for the binding to wrap over the quilt layers and cover the machine stitching, without me having to yank and stretch my fabric.

1. Cut the number of binding strips indicated in the project instructions, cutting across the width of the fabric. With right sides together, join the strips end to end at right angles to make one long strip. Trim the seam allowances to ¼" and press the seam allowances open.

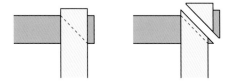

2. Cut the beginning of the binding strip at a 45° angle. Press this end under ¼".

3. Press the binding strip in half, wrong sides together.

4. Position the beginning of the binding strip on one side of the quilt back (preferably the bottom edge), aligning the raw edges. Using a ¼" seam allowance, begin stitching about 12" from the end of the binding. Stop stitching ¼" from the corner. Leave the needle down.

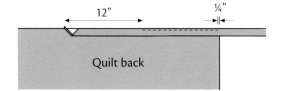

5. Turn the quilt clockwise so the corner is pointing toward you. Sew into the corner and off the binding. Remove the needle from the quilt and cut the threads.

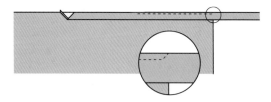

6. Fold the binding up and then back down so that the binding and quilt raw edges are aligned. You will have a fold at the top of the binding.

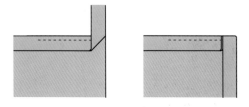

7. Begin stitching at the fold of the binding and stop when you are ¼" from the corner, leaving the needle down. Repeat steps 5 and 6. Repeat the stitching and mitering process on the remaining edges and corners of the quilt.

8. When you have turned the last corner, stop about 2" from the beginning of the binding with the needle in the fabric. Trim the end of the binding strip so it overlaps the beginning of the binding strip 2" to 3". Tuck the end into the beginning and continue stitching the binding to the top.

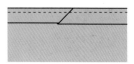

9. Fold the binding to the front over the raw edges, covering the machine stitching. Using a zigzag stitch (other stitches, such as a blind hem stitch or straight stitch will also work) and thread that matches the binding, stitch the edge of the binding in place, mitering the corners.

Dancing WITH THE FLOWERS

Take a traditional block and supersize it for a dynamic quilt in bold, large-scale prints. No need to "fussy cut" the flowers. Let your rotary cutter make the decision for you. Don't be afraid of the mitered stripes around the center square. I'll let you in on my secret method for this and you'll never want to use the traditional Y-seam method again!

Block Finished Size: 20" x 20" ■ Number of Blocks in Quilt: 4 ■ Quilt Finished Size: 76" x 76"

MATERIALS

Yardages are based on 42"-wide fabrics.

2⅜ yards of large-scale green floral for outer border

1 yard of large-scale brown floral for blocks and sashing squares

1 yard of multicolored striped fabric for blocks and inner border

1 yard of green dot print for sashing

⅝ yard of cream print for blocks

⅝ yard of rust print for blocks

½ yard of pink floral for sashing

⅝ yard of fabric for binding

4½ yards of fabric for backing

84" x 84" square of batting

CUTTING

From the large-scale brown floral, cut:
4 squares, 10½" x 10½"
2 strips, 6½" x 42"; crosscut into 9 squares, 6½" x 6½"

From the multicolored striped fabric, cut:
16 strips, 2½" x 15"
6 strips, 1½" x 42"

From the cream print, cut:
3 strips, 5⅞" x 42"; crosscut into 16 squares, 5⅞" x 5⅞". Cut each square once diagonally to yield 32 triangles.

From the rust print, cut:
3 strips, 5½" x 42"; crosscut into 16 squares, 5½" x 5½"

From the pink floral, cut:
6 strips, 2½" x 42"

From the green dot print, cut:
12 strips, 2½" x 42"

From the *lengthwise grain* of the large-scale green floral, cut:
4 strips, 8½" x 78"

From the fabric for binding, cut:
8 strips, 2⅛" x 42"

Designed and sewn by Debby Kratovil; machine quilted by Abigail Dolinger.

MAKING THE BLOCKS

① Center a striped 2½" x 15" strip on one side of a brown floral 10½" square. Sew from the edge of the square to the opposite edge. Press the seam allowance *toward* the square. Repeat on the opposite side of the square.

② Center a striped 2½" x 15" strip on each of the remaining sides of the square. Sew the pieces in place, beginning and ending ¼" from the ends of the square, in the seams of the previously sewn strips. Your stitches should not capture any of the first two strips. Press the seam allowances *away from* the center square.

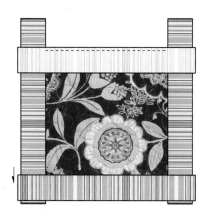

③ Fold under the ends of the last two strips you added so they form a 45° angle (miter) at each corner. Pin down the angled edge and blindstitch it in place by machine or hand. If you choose to machine stitch, monofilament thread is a good choice for this task. Trim away the excess fabric from the four corners on the wrong side of the unit, leaving a ¼" seam allowance. Press well.

④ Repeat steps 1–3 to make a total of four block center units measuring 14½" square.

⑤ Sew a cream triangle to adjacent sides of a rust 5½" square. Press the seam allowances toward the triangles. Repeat to make a total of 16 block-corner units.

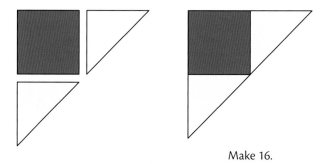

Make 16.

⑥ Sew a corner unit to opposite sides of a center unit. Press the seam allowances toward the center unit. Repeat on the remaining sides of the unit. Repeat to make a total of four blocks measuring 20½" square.

Make 4.

MAKING THE SASHING UNITS

Sew a pink strip between two green dot strips to make a strip set. Press the seam allowances toward the green fabric. Repeat to make a total of six strip sets. Crosscut the strip sets into 12 segments, 20½" wide.

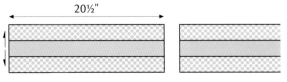

20½"

Make 6 strip sets.
Cut 12 segments.

ASSEMBLING THE QUILT TOP

1. Alternately sew three brown floral 6½" squares and two sashing units together. Repeat to make a total of three sashing rows.

Make 3.

2. Alternately sew three sashing units and two blocks together. Repeat to make a total of two block rows.

Make 2.

3. Refer to the quilt-assembly diagram to alternately sew the sashing and block rows together. The quilt center should now measure 58½" square.

4. Cut two of the striped 1½" x 42" inner-border strips in half crosswise to make four strips 1½" x 21". Sew one of these strips to each of the remaining four striped strips to create four inner-border strips.

5. Measure the quilt top through the center from side to side and cut two inner-border strips to this measurement. Sew the strips to the top and bottom edges of the quilt top. Press the seam

allowances toward the borders. Measure the quilt top through the center from top to bottom, including the borders, and cut the remaining two inner-border strips to this measurement. Sew the strips to the sides of the quilt top. Press the seam allowances toward the borders.

6. Refer to "Magical Mitered Corners" on page 10 to sew the green floral 8½"-wide border strips to the quilt top.

Quilt assembly

FINISHING THE QUILT

1. Prepare a quilt backing that is 6" longer and wider than the quilt top.

2. Layer the backing, batting, and quilt top. Pin, hand baste, or spray baste the layers together.

3. Quilt using your preferred method. Trim the excess batting and backing even with the edges of the quilt top.

4. Using the 2⅛"-wide binding strips, make and attach the binding, referring to page 10 as needed.

PRINCESS *Feather*

I love the timeless beauty of antique blocks like the Princess Feather, but I like to give them my own touch. This mid-nineteenth-century design beckoned me to enlarge it and go wild with bold colors. I couldn't resist the unorthodox mix of colors, and as a result I have one quilt that never fails to bring a smile to my face. The appliqué technique has been updated, too; no hand stitching for me—I love my sewing machines too much!

Block Finished Size: 30" x 30" ■ Number of Blocks in Quilt: 1 ■ Quilt Finished Size: 44" x 44"

MATERIALS

Yardages are based on 42"-wide fabrics.

1 yard of dark khaki solid for block background

⅞ yard of black floral for wreath feather appliqués and pieced border

⅞ yard of blue print for wreath feather appliqués, pieced-border corner squares, and binding

½ yard of black striped fabric for pieced border

½ yard of orange-and-red print for corner feather appliqués and pieced border

5" x 5" square of dark pink print for center star appliqué

3 yards of fabric for backing

52" x 52" square of batting

1½ yards of 18"-wide paper-backed fusible web

Threads for machine appliqué

Freezer paper

CUTTING

From the fusible web, cut:

1 square, 5" x 5"

12 rectangles, 4" x 6"

8 rectangles, 6" x 7"

From the blue print, cut:

1 strip, 6" x 42"; crosscut into 8 rectangles, 4" x 6"

1 strip, 7½" x 42"; crosscut into 4 squares, 7½" x 7½"

5 strips, 2⅛" x 42"

From the black floral, cut:

2 strips, 6" x 42"; crosscut into 8 rectangles, 6" x 7"

4 strips, 3¼" x 30½"

From the orange-and-red print, cut:

1 strip, 6" x 42"; crosscut into 4 rectangles, 4" x 6"

4 strips, 2" x 30½"

From the dark khaki solid, cut:

1 square, 32" x 32"

From the black striped fabric, cut:

4 strips, 3¼" x 30½"

Designed and sewn by Debby Kratovil; machine quilted by Cathy MacDonald.

PREPARING THE APPLIQUÉS

① Follow the manufacturer's instructions to adhere the fusible-web pieces to the wrong side of the corresponding dark pink square and blue, black floral, and orange-and-red rectangles. Do not remove the paper from the fusible web after you have fused the pieces to the fabrics.

② Trace each of the patterns on page 19 onto freezer paper and cut them out. Iron the templates to the right side of the fused pieces from step 1 as follows: center star template to the dark pink square, wreath feather bottom/corner templates to a blue rectangle, and wreath feather top to a black floral rectangle. Cut out each shape. Remove the freezer-paper template and fusible-web paper from each shape. Using the freezer-paper templates that you just removed, repeat this process to cut out a total of eight feather top appliqués from the remaining black floral rectangles, a total of eight feather bottom appliqués from the remaining blue rectangles, and a total of four corner feather appliqués from the remaining orange-and-red rectangles.

MAKING THE BLOCK

① To aid in the placement of the appliqués, finger-press the dark khaki square in half vertically, horizontally, and diagonally in both directions.

② Center the star in the middle of the square and pin it in place. Using the finger-pressed lines, arrange the wreath feather bottom appliqués as shown and pin them in place. Next, place the wreath feather top appliqués along the pressed lines, tucking the pointed end of the feather tops under the feather bottoms about ¼"; pin them in place. Position the pointed end of each corner feather 2" in from each background corner, aligning them with the diagonally pressed lines; pin them in place. Once you are satisfied with the position of all of the

appliqués, fuse them in place, following the manufacturer's instructions.

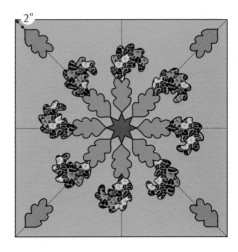

③ Stitch around the edges of each appliqué to secure them in place, working from the center appliqué outward. I prefer to use a variegated-color thread and a narrow zigzag stitch, but other thread colors and stitches also could be used.

④ Press the block well. Trim it to 30½" x 30½", keeping the design centered.

MAKING AND ADDING THE PIECED BORDER

① Sew an orange-and-red strip between a black striped strip and a black floral strip. Press the seam allowances toward the black strips. Repeat to make a total of four pieced borders.

Make 4.

② Referring to the photo on page 17, sew a pieced border to the sides of the quilt top. Press the seam allowances toward the borders. Add a blue square to the ends of the remaining two pieced borders. Press the seam allowances toward the squares. Sew these borders to the top and bottom of the quilt top. Press the seam allowances toward the borders.

FINISHING THE QUILT

1. Prepare a quilt backing that is 6" longer and wider than the quilt top.

2. Layer the backing, batting, and quilt top. Pin, hand baste, or spray baste the layers together.

3. Quilt, using your preferred method. Trim the excess batting and backing even with the edges of the quilt top.

4. Using the blue 2⅛"-wide strips, make and attach the binding, referring to page 10 as needed.

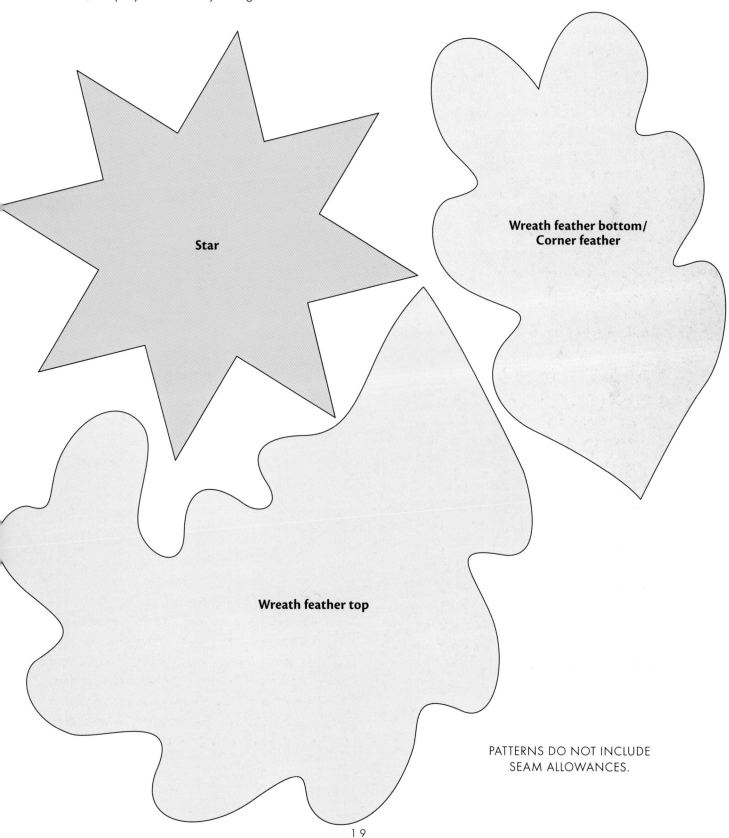

Star

Wreath feather bottom/
Corner feather

Wreath feather top

PATTERNS DO NOT INCLUDE
SEAM ALLOWANCES.

Glorious BLOOMS

Let the flowers sing! Bright, bold blooms cry out for a large space to strut their stuff. I tried to capture the rich colors of the main floral print without having it upstaged by competing prints. Surrounding the center squares of each block with calm, yet beautiful prints allowed me to do just that.

Block Finished Size: 20" x 20" ▪ Number of Blocks in Quilt: 4 ▪ Quilt Finished Size: 46" x 46"

MATERIALS

¾ yard of floral on black background fabric for blocks

¾ yard of cream tone-on-tone print for block backgrounds

⅝ yard of green print for blocks

⅝ yard of purple print for blocks

½ yard of multicolored striped fabric for border

¼ yard of small-scale lavender print for block corners and pieced border

¼ yard of red small-scale rose print for block corners and pieced border

⅜ yard of black print for binding

3 yards of fabric for backing

52" x 52" piece of batting

CUTTING

From the floral on black background fabric, cut:

4 squares, 11½" x 11½"

From the green print, cut:

4 strips, 2" x 42"; crosscut into:

    4 strips, 2" x 11½"

    4 strips, 2" x 14½"

2 squares, 7¼" x 7¼"; cut twice diagonally to yield 8 quarter-square triangles

From the purple print, cut:

4 strips, 2" x 42"; crosscut into:

    4 strips, 2" x 11½"

    4 strips, 2" x 14½"

2 squares, 7¼" x 7¼"; cut twice diagonally to yield 8 quarter-square triangles

From the cream tone-on-tone print, cut:

2 strips, 3⅞" x 42"; crosscut into 16 squares, 3⅞" x 3⅞". Cut each square once diagonally to yield 32 half-square triangles.

4 strips, 3½" x 42"; crosscut into 32 rectangles, 3½" x 4½"

From the rose print, cut:

2 strips, 3½" x 42"; crosscut into 18 squares, 3½" x 3½"

From the small-scale lavender print, cut:

2 strips, 3½" x 42"; crosscut into 18 squares, 3½" x 3½"

From the multicolored striped fabric, cut:

4 strips, 3½" x 42"; crosscut into 8 strips, 3½" x 14½"

From the black print, cut:

5 strips, 2⅛" x 42"

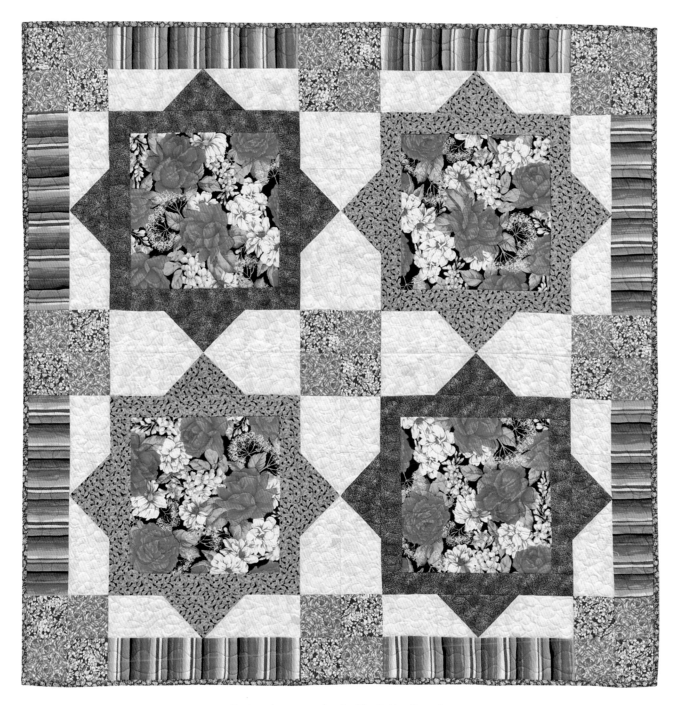

Designed, sewn, and quilted by Debby Kratovil.

MAKING THE BLOCKS

1. Sew a green 2" x 11½" strip to opposite sides of two floral 11½" squares. Press the seam allowances toward the strips. Sew a green 2" x 14½" strip to the remaining two sides of the squares. Press the seam allowances toward the strips. Repeat with the purple strips on the other two floral squares to make a total of two green and two purple framed squares measuring 14½" square.

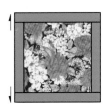

Make 2.

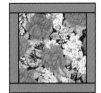

Make 2.

2. Sew a cream triangle to the short sides of each green and each purple triangle to make flying-geese units. Press the seam allowances toward the cream triangles.

Make 8.

Make 8.

3. Sew a cream rectangle to the short ends of each green and each purple flying-geese unit. Press the seam allowances toward the cream rectangles.

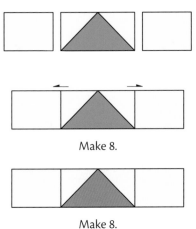

Make 8.

Make 8.

4. Sew a green flying-geese unit from step 3 to opposite sides of each green framed square from step 1. Press the seam allowances toward the green strips. Join a rose square to the ends of the remaining four flying-geese units. Press the seam allowances toward the squares. Sew these strips to the top and bottom of the green framed squares to make two green blocks measuring 20½" square. Press the seam allowances toward the green strips. Repeat with the purple framed squares, the purple flying-geese units, and the lavender squares to make two purple blocks.

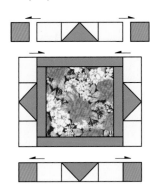
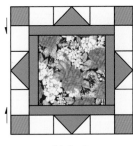

Make 2.

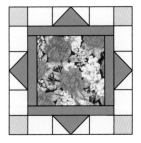

Make 2.

ASSEMBLING THE QUILT TOP

1. Sew a green block to a purple block to make a row. Repeat to make a total of two rows. Press the seam allowances of each row in the same direction.

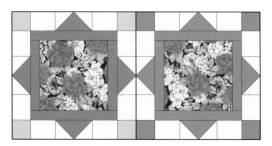

Make 2.

2. Refer to the quilt-assembly diagram to join the blocks rows, alternating the block colors. Press the seam allowance in either direction.

3. Sew a rose square to the ends of four striped strips. Press the seam allowances toward the strips. Repeat to sew a lavender square to the ends of the remaining four striped strips.

Make 4.

Make 4.

4. Join each strip with rose squares to the end of a strip with lavender squares to make a pieced border strip.

Make 4.

5. Refer to the quilt-assembly diagram to join a pieced border strip to opposite sides of the quilt top so the rose and lavender squares alternate. Press

the seam allowances toward the borders. Join a lavender square to the rose ends of the remaining two pieced border strips and a rose square to the lavender ends. Press the seam allowances away from the newly added squares. Sew these strips to the top and bottom of the quilt top. Press the seam allowances toward the borders.

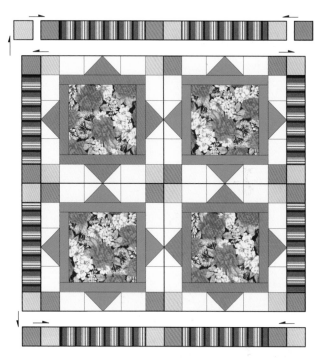

Quilt assembly

FINISHING THE QUILT

1. Prepare a quilt backing that is 6" longer and wider than the quilt top.

2. Layer the backing, batting, and quilt top. Pin, hand baste, or spray baste the layers together.

3. Quilt using your preferred method. Trim the excess batting and backing even with the edges of the quilt top.

4. Using the black strips, make and attach the binding, referring to page 10 as needed.

JEWELED *Crazy* HEARTS

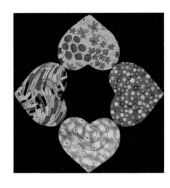

My friend Jan Jolly loves hearts and bright colors, so when she saw a package of precut bright hearts, she had to have them. Once she had them, however, she didn't know what to do with them, so they sat untouched for more than a year. Inspiration for using the hearts came while visiting a quilt shop in South Carolina when she was on a sewing vacation with a friend. It was there that she decided to just appliqué them onto a solid piece of fabric. From there, the layout was decided, and a quilt was born. The finishing touch was to use an extra-wide binding that acts as a border.

Whole-Cloth Quilt Finished Size: 42" x 42"

MATERIALS

Yardages are based on 42"-wide fabrics.

1⅜ yards of black print for background

64 squares, 4½" x 4½", of assorted bright prints (or a purchased package of precut 4" hearts)

¾ yard of multicolored print for binding

2 yards of fabric for backing

48" x 48" square of batting

2¼ yards of 18"-wide paper-backed fusible web

Freezer paper

Thread for machine appliqué (black was used for this quilt, but a multicolored variegated thread would also work nicely)

Light-colored marking pencil

CUTTING

From the fusible web, cut:
64 squares, 4½" x 4½"

From the black print, cut:
1 square, 42" x 42"

From the multicolored print, cut:
5 strips, 4½" x 42"

PREPARING THE APPLIQUÉS

1. Follow the manufacturer's instructions to adhere the fusible-web squares to the wrong side of each bright square. Do not remove the paper from the fusible web after you have fused it to the squares.

2. Trace the pattern on page 27 onto freezer paper and cut it out. Iron the template to the right side of one of the fused squares from step 1 and cut it out. Remove the freezer paper template from the square. Using the freezer-paper template that you just removed, repeat this process with the remaining

Designed and sewn by Jan Jolly; machine quilted by Silvia Davis.

fused squares. The template can be used over and over again, but if you notice that it isn't adhering well after several uses, cut another one from a new piece of freezer paper.

PREPARING THE BACKGROUND

Using a white or light-colored marking pencil, mark a 1" seam allowance around the outer edges of the black print square. Divide the area inside the seam allowance markings into four vertical and four horizontal rows, each 10" wide.

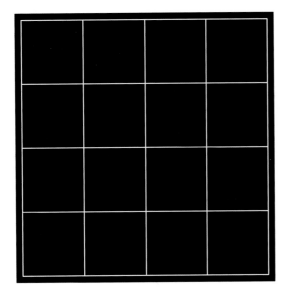

APPLIQUÉING THE HEARTS

1 Randomly select four heart shapes and carefully remove the paper backing from each. Arrange the hearts, right side up, inside one marked square on the right side of the black background, with the tip of one heart centered on each side of the marked square. When all four hearts are in place,

follow the manufacturer's instructions to fuse them in place. Repeat for each of the remaining marked squares on the background.

Appliqué placement

2 Stitch around the edges of each heart to secure it in place, working outward from the center of the quilt top. I prefer to use a simple zigzag stitch, but other stitches also could be used.

FINISHING THE QUILT

1 Prepare a quilt backing that is 6" longer and wider than the quilt top.

2 Layer the backing, batting, and quilt top. Pin, hand baste, or spray baste the layers together.

3 Quilt, using your preferred method. Trim the excess batting and backing even with the edges of the quilt top.

4 On the quilt backing, use a white or light-colored marking pencil to mark a line ¾" from the edges around the perimeter of the quilt. Refer to "Machine Stitched Binding" on page 10 to prepare the 4½"-wide binding strips. Align the raw edges of the binding strip with the marked line and attach it as you normally would. You should be stitching on the outer perimeter line that you previously marked on the quilt top. Be sure you are not catching the tips of the heart appliqués.

Heart

PATTERN DOES NOT INCLUDE
SEAM ALLOWANCE.

Snow CRYSTALS

Snow Crystals is a traditional pattern sewn in a nontraditional manner. There are no set-in seams; it's all straight-seam sewing. Easy foundation-piecing techniques make this 24" block a joy to create.

Block Finished Size: 24" x 24" ■ Number of Blocks in Quilt: 1 ■ Quilt Finished Size: 34" x 34"

MATERIALS

Yardages are based on 42"-wide fabrics.

1⅛ yards of blue print for block star points, outer border, and binding

⅝ yard of light print for block background

½ yard of orange print for block star points and inner border

¼ yard of green print for block star points

¼ yard of pink print for block star points

1¼ yards of fabric for backing

40" x 40" square of batting

Foundation paper

CUTTING

From the blue print, cut:
2 strips, 3" x 42"; crosscut into 8 rectangles, 3" x 8"
4 strips, 4½" x 42"
4 strips, 2⅛" x 42"

From the green print, cut:
2 strips, 3" x 42"; crosscut into 8 rectangles, 3" x 8"

From the pink print, cut:
2 strips, 3" x 42"; crosscut into 8 rectangles, 3" x 8"

From the orange print, cut:
2 strips, 3" x 42"; crosscut into 8 rectangles, 3" x 8"
4 strips, 1½" x 42"

From the light print, cut:
4 strips, 4½" x 42"; crosscut into 32 squares, 4½" x 4½". Cut each square once diagonally to yield 64 triangles.

Designed, sewn, and quilted by Debby Kratovil.

MAKING THE BLOCK

Refer to "Paper Piecing" on page 7 for paper-piecing specifics.

1. Make 16 copies *each* of units A and B on page 31 using your preferred method. Each quadrant of the Snow Crystals block uses one A and one B foundation. Remember, patterns are the mirror image of the finished block or unit.

2. Paper piece each unit, using the blue, green, pink, and orange rectangles and the light triangles where indicated on the foundations. Trim away any excess fabric extending beyond the outer line of each unit.

Make 8 of each.   Make 8 of each.

3. Join each pink unit to a blue unit, and each green unit to an orange unit as shown. Press the seam allowances open.

Make 8.   Make 8.

4. Lay out and assemble the joined units as shown to make sections A and B. Make two of each section. Remove the paper foundations. Press the seam allowances open. Each section should measure 12½" square.

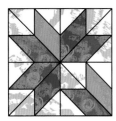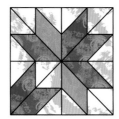

Section A.   Section B.
Make 2.   Make 2.

5. Sew the four sections together as shown to create the Snow Crystals block. The block should now measure 24½" square.

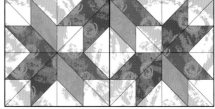

ASSEMBLING THE QUILT TOP

1. Measure the block through the center from top to bottom and cut two orange 1½" x 42" inner-border strips to this measurement. Sew the strips to the sides of the block. Press the seam allowances toward the borders. Measure the block through the center from side to side, including the borders, and cut the remaining two orange strips to this measurement. Sew the strips to the top and bottom edges of the block. Press the seam allowances toward the borders.

2. Repeat step 1 with the blue 4½" x 42" strips to add the outer borders.

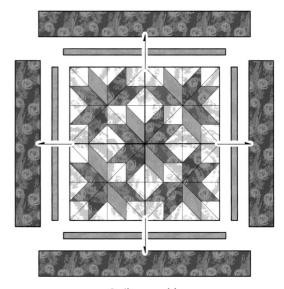

Quilt assembly

FINISHING THE QUILT

1. Prepare a quilt backing that is 6" longer and wider than the quilt top.

2. Layer the backing, batting, and quilt top. Pin, hand baste, or spray baste the layers together.

3. Quilt using your preferred method. Trim the excess batting and backing even with the edges of the quilt top.

4. Using the blue 2⅛"-wide strips, make and attach the binding, referring to page 10 as needed.

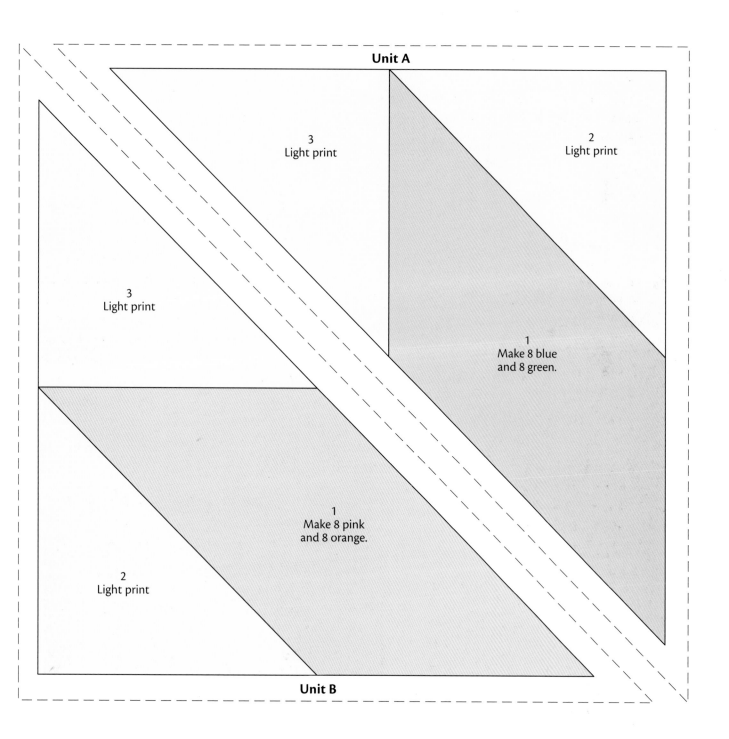

Unit A

3
Light print

2
Light print

3
Light print

1
Make 8 blue
and 8 green.

1
Make 8 pink
and 8 orange.

2
Light print

Unit B

Diamond HEAD

The inspiration for this quilt comes from a block by Judy Martin, called Diamond Head. Her block uses a true diamond shape, however, and mine uses a parallelogram. It's really a traditional Windmill block set on point. The border print gave me permission to use a very unusual color combination—orange and grape. Yummm! Paper piecing the block centers makes for very sharp star points.

Block Finished Size: 17" x 17" ■ Number of Blocks in Quilt: 4 ■ Quilt Finished Size: 51½" x 51½"

MATERIALS

Yardages are based on 42"-wide fabrics.

2 yards of large-scale floral for border and binding

1 yard of orange print for block background

⅔ yard of grape solid

⅜ yard of grape striped fabric

⅓ yard mustard-and-grape striped fabric for inner border

58" x 58" square of batting

3½ yards of fabric for backing

CUTTING

From the orange print, cut:

1 strip, 9¾" x 42"; crosscut into 4 squares, 9¾" x 9¾". Cut each square twice diagonally to yield 16 quarter-square triangles.

4 strips, 3" x 42"; crosscut into 16 rectangles, 3" x 8"

2 strips, 4½" x 42"; crosscut into 16 squares, 4½" x 4½". Cut each square once diagonally to yield 32 half-square triangles.

From the grape solid, cut:

4 strips, 3" x 42"; crosscut into 16 rectangles, 3" x 8"

2 strips, 4½" x 42"; crosscut into 16 squares, 4½" x 4½". Cut each square once diagonally to yield 32 half-square triangles.

From the grape striped fabric, cut:

1 strip, 9¾" x 42"; crosscut into 4 squares, 9¾" x 9¾". Cut each square twice diagonally to yield 16 quarter-square triangles.

From the mustard-and-grape striped fabric, cut:

4 strips, 1¾" x 42"

From the large-scale floral, cut:

6 strips, 2⅛" x 42"

From the *lengthwise grain* of the remaining large-scale floral, cut:

2 strips, 8" x 38"

2 strips, 8" x 53"

MAKING THE BLOCK

Refer to "Paper Piecing" on page 7 for paper-piecing specifics.

1 Make 16 copies *each* of units A and B on page 35 using your preferred method. Each quadrant of the Diamond Head block uses one A and one B foundation. Remember, patterns are the mirror image of the finished block or unit.

Designed and sewn by Debby Kratovil; quilted by Cathy MacDonald.

2 Paper piece each unit, using the orange and grape solid rectangles and half-square triangles where indicated on the foundations. Trim away any excess fabric extending beyond the outer line of each unit.

Unit A.
Make 16.

Unit B.
Make 16.

3 Join each A unit to a B unit as shown. Press the seam allowances open.

Make 16.

4 Lay out and assemble four units from step 3 as shown, pressing the seam allowances open. Repeat to make a total of four block centers measuring 12½" square. Remove the paper foundations.

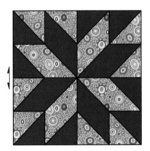

Make 4.

5 Sew each grape striped quarter-square triangle to an orange quarter-square triangle. Press the seam allowances open.

Make 16.

6 Sew a triangle unit from step 5 to each side of a block center unit from step 4, sewing opposite sides

first. Press the seam allowances toward the triangle units. The blocks should now measure 17½" square.

Make 4.

ASSEMBLING THE QUILT TOP

1 Refer to the quilt assembly diagram to lay out the blocks in two rows of two blocks each. Sew the blocks in each row together. Press the seam allowances open. Sew the rows together. Press the seam allowances open. The quilt top should now measure 34½" square.

2 Measure the quilt top through the center from side to side and trim two mustard-and-grape striped inner-border strips to this measurement. Sew the strips to the top and bottom edges of the quilt top. Press the seam allowances toward the borders. Measure the quilt top through the center from top to bottom, including the borders, and cut the remaining two mustard-and-grape strips to this measurement. Sew the strips to the sides of the quilt top. Press the seam allowances toward the borders.

3 Repeat step 2 with the floral 8"-wide strips, trimming the 38"-long strips to fit the top and bottom edges and the 53"-long strips to fit the sides.

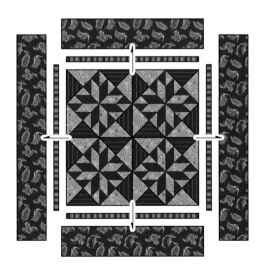

Quilt assembly

FINISHING THE QUILT

1 Prepare a quilt backing that is 6" longer and wider than the quilt top.

2 Layer the backing, batting, and quilt top. Pin, hand baste, or spray baste the layers together.

3 Quilt using your preferred method. Trim the excess batting and backing even with the edges of the quilt top.

4 Using the floral 2⅛"-wide strips, make and attach the binding, referring to page 10 as needed.

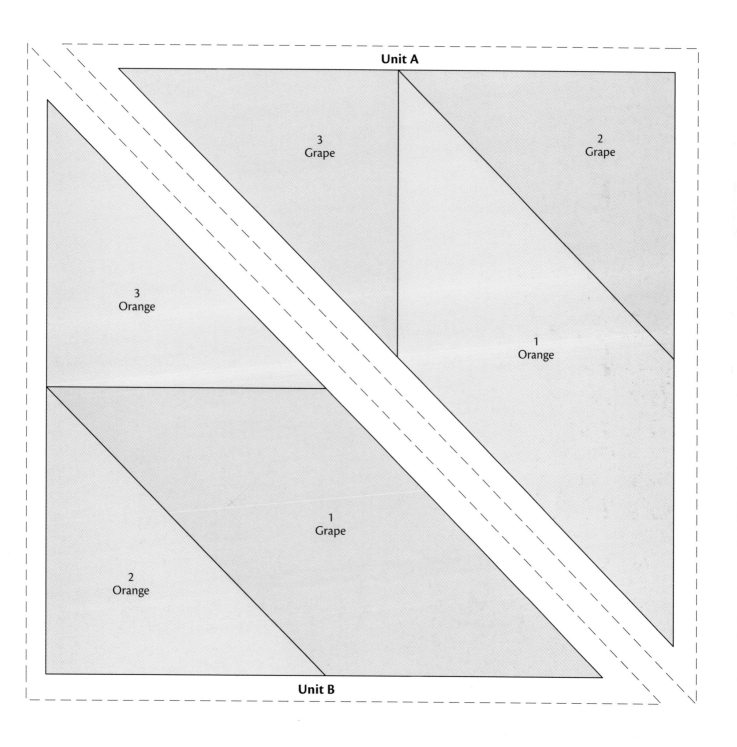

Unit A

3
Grape

2
Grape

3
Orange

1
Orange

1
Grape

2
Orange

Unit B

Peacock GARDEN

Just a simple four-patch unit set on point becomes quite a showstopper when the fabrics take their inspiration from the colorful plumes of a peacock strutting in a lush, green garden. My original design using six big blocks had to change when I ran out of fabric. Not to worry, I told myself. The half blocks create an interesting center, and I was finished with the quilt sooner.

Block Finished Size: 21½" x 21½"
Number of Blocks in Quilt: 4 whole blocks, 2 half blocks ■ Quilt Finished Size: 72" x 86¾"

MATERIALS

Yardages are based on 42"-wide fabrics.

3 yards of magenta peacock feather print for blocks and outer border

1½ yards of green floral for blocks and sashing

1⅛ yards of green geometric print for block backgrounds and sashing squares

1⅛ yards of lavender print for block backgrounds and inner border

⅞ yard of magenta dot print for sashing

⅔ yard of magenta plaid for binding

5½ yards of fabric for backing

80" x 95" piece of batting

CUTTING

From the magenta peacock feather print, cut:
5 strips, 4¼" x 42"

From the *lengthwise grain* of the remaining magenta peacock feather print, cut:
4 strips, 8" x 74"

From the green floral, cut:
5 strips, 4¼" x 42"

1 strip, 22" x 42"; crosscut into 14 strips, 2½" x 22"

3 strips, 2½" x 11¼"

From the green geometric print, cut:
4 strips, 6¼" x 42"; crosscut into 20 squares, 6¼" x 6¼". Cut each square once diagonally to yield 40 triangles.

2 strips, 4½" x 42"; crosscut into 12 squares, 4½" x 4½"

From the lavender print, cut:
4 strips, 6¼" x 42"; crosscut into 20 squares, 6¼" x 6¼". Cut each square once diagonally to yield 40 triangles.

7 strips, 1½" x 42"

From the magenta dot print, cut:
1 strip, 22" x 42"; crosscut into 14 strips, 2½" x 22"

3 strips, 2½" x 11¼"

From the magenta plaid, cut:
9 strips, 2⅛" x 42"

Designed and sewn by Debby Kratovil; machine quilted by Cathy MacDonald.

MAKING THE BLOCKS

1 Join a magenta peacock 4¼" x 42" strip to a green floral 4¼" x 42" strip to make a strip set. Repeat to make a total of five strip sets. Press the seam allowances toward the magenta strips. Crosscut the strip sets into 40 segments, 4¼" wide.

4¼"

Make 5 strip sets.
Cut 40 segments.

2 Sew two strip-set segments together as shown to make a four-patch unit. Repeat to make a total of 20 units measuring 8" square.

Make 20.

3 Sew a green geometric-print triangle to opposite sides of each four-patch unit, being careful to orient the triangles on the unit as shown. Press the seam allowances toward the triangles. Sew a lavender triangle to the remaining sides of each unit. Press the seam allowance toward the triangles. Trim the units ¼" away from the points of the four-patch units so that they measure 11¼" square.

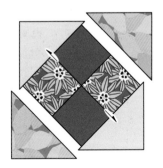

Make 20.

4 Sew two units from step 3 together, positioning the green triangles in the upper-left and lower-right corners. Repeat to make a total of 10 pairs. Press the seam allowance open.

Make 10.

5 Sew two pairs together. Press the seam allowances open. Repeat to make a total of four blocks measuring 22" square. The remaining two pairs are the half blocks.

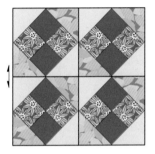

Make 4.

MAKING THE SASHING AND BLOCK ROWS

1 Sew a magenta dot 2½" x 11¼" strip to each green floral 2½" x 11¼" strip to make 3 short sashing strips. Press the seam allowances toward the magenta strips. Repeat with the magenta dot and green floral 2½" x 22" strips to make 14 long sashing strips.

Make 3.

Make 14.

2 Alternately sew three green geometric-print 4½" squares and two long sashing strips together to make a sashing row, being careful that the colors alternate positions as shown in the two variations.

Make two rows of each variation. Press the seam allowances toward the sashing strips.

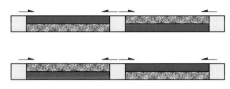

Make 2 of each.

③ Alternately join three long sashing strips and two whole blocks, being careful to position the sashing strips as shown. Press the seam allowances toward the strips. Repeat to make a total of two whole block rows.

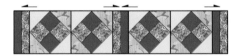

Make 2.

④ Make one half block row using the two half blocks and remaining three short sashing strips, again being careful to position the sashing strips as shown. Press the seam allowances toward the strips.

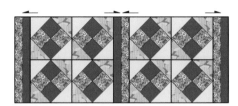

Make 1.

ASSEMBLING THE QUILT TOP

① Refer to the quilt-assembly diagram to alternately sew the sashing rows and block rows together, being careful to position the sashing colors as shown. Press the seam allowances toward the sashing rows. The quilt top should now measure 55½" x 70¼".

② Piece the lavender 1½" x 42" strips together end to end to make one long strip. Measure the quilt top through the center from side to side. From the pieced strip, cut two strips to this measure-ment. Sew the strips to the top and bottom of the quilt top. Press the seam allowances toward the borders. Measure the quilt top through the center from top to bottom, including the borders. From the remainder of the pieced strip, cut two strips to this measurement. Sew the strips to the sides of the quilt top. Press the seam allowances toward the borders.

③ Repeat step 2 with the magenta peacock 8"-wide strips to add the outer border.

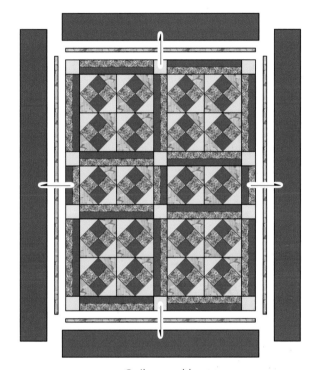

Quilt assembly

FINISHING THE QUILT

① Prepare a quilt backing that is 6" longer and wider than the quilt top.

② Layer the backing, batting, and quilt top. Pin, hand baste, or spray baste the layers together.

③ Quilt using your preferred method. Trim the excess batting and backing even with the edges of the quilt top.

④ Using the magenta plaid strips, make and attach the binding, referring to page 10 as needed.

Asian ALLEGORY

The large area in the center of this block makes it the perfect place to showcase a fabulous fabric with a large-scale print. The magnificent floral print with gilded etchings that I chose reminds me of a print that might be found on antique Chinese paper.

Block Finished Size: 16" x 16" ■ Number of Blocks in Quilt: 4 ■ Quilt Finished Size: 55" x 55"

MATERIALS

Yardages are based on 42"-wide fabrics.

2 yards of large-scale pink-and-blue floral for block centers and outer border

½ yard of green-and-pink print for sashing

⅜ yard of black solid for blocks and sashing squares

⅜ yard of blue print for blocks

⅓ yard of multicolored (red, pink, and black) floral for blocks

¼ yard of olive green print 1 for inner border

¼ yard of olive green print 2 for blocks

¼ yard of ivory print for blocks

¼ yard of red print for blocks

½ yard of pink-and-navy print for binding

3½ yards of fabric for backing

62" x 62" square of batting

CUTTING

From the black solid, cut:
4 strips, 2½" x 42"; crosscut into 57 squares, 2½" x 2½"

From the olive green print 2, cut:
1 strip, 2½" x 42"; crosscut into 16 squares, 2½" x 2½"

From the multicolored (red, pink, and black) floral, cut:
2 strips, 4½" x 42"; crosscut into 16 squares, 4½" x 4½"

From the blue print, cut:
4 strips, 2½" x 42"; crosscut into 16 rectangles, 2½" x 8½"

From the ivory print, cut:
2 strips, 2½" x 42"; crosscut into 8 rectangles, 2½" x 8½"

From the red print, cut:
2 strips, 2½" x 42"; crosscut into 8 rectangles, 2½" x 8½"

From the *lengthwise grain* of the large-scale pink-and-blue floral, cut:
2 strips, 8" x 42"
2 strips, 8" x 58"
4 squares, 8½" x 8½"

From the green-and-pink print, cut:
6 strips, 2½" x 42"; crosscut into 12 strips, 2½" x 16½"

From the olive green print 1, cut:
4 strips, 1½" x 42"

From the pink-and-navy print, cut:
6 strips, 2⅛" x 42"

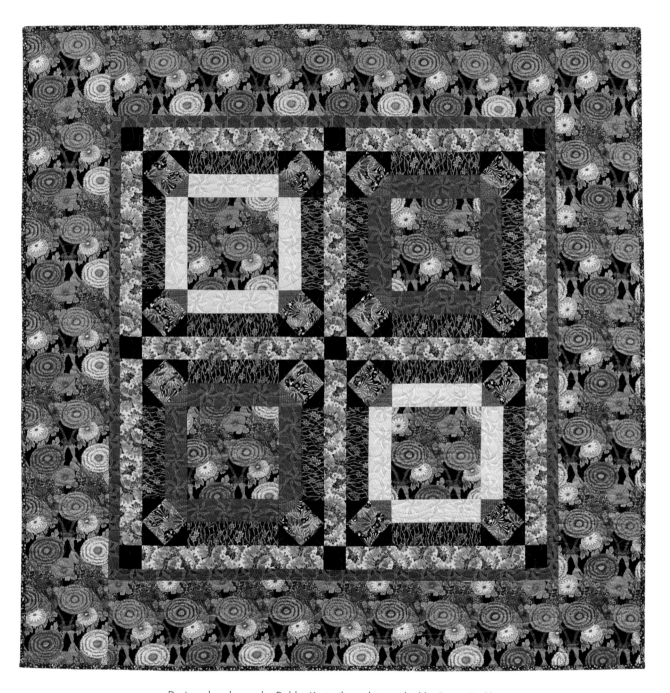

Designed and sewn by Debby Kratovil; machine quilted by Peggy Barkle.

MAKING THE BLOCKS

1 Draw a diagonal line from corner to corner on the wrong side of 48 black squares (a No. 2 lead pencil is a good marking tool for black fabric) and each of the olive green 2 squares.

2 Position a marked black square on opposite corners of a multicolored square as shown. Sew on the marked lines. Trim ¼" from the line. Press the resulting triangles outward. Place a marked black square and a marked olive green 2 square on the remaining two corners of the multicolored square. Sew, trim, and press as before. Repeat to make a total of 16 square-in-a-square units.

Make 16.

3 Sew a blue rectangle to each ivory rectangle and to each red rectangle along the long edges to make pieced rectangles. Press the seam allowances open.

Make 8 of each.

4 Arrange one large-scale floral square, four square-in-a-square units, and four blue-and-ivory pieced rectangles into three horizontal rows as shown. Be sure the green triangle of the square-in-a-square units is pointed toward the center square. Sew the pieces in each row together. Press the seam allowances toward the pieced rectangles. Sew the rows together. Press the seam allowances open. Repeat

with the remaining floral squares, square-in-a-square units, and pieced rectangles to make a total of two blue-and-ivory blocks and two blue-and-red blocks.

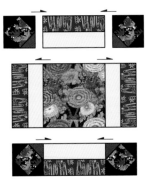 

Make 2.

Make 2.

ASSEMBLING THE QUILT TOP

1 Alternately join three black squares and two green-and-pink sashing strips. Press the seam allowances toward the strips. Repeat to make a total of three sashing rows.

Make 3.

2 Alternately join three green-and-pink sashing strips, one blue-and-ivory block, and one blue-and-red block. Press the seam allowances toward the strips. Repeat to make a total of two block rows.

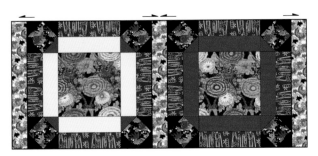

Make 2.

3 Refer to the quilt assembly diagram to alternately sew the sashing rows and block rows together. Press the seam allowances toward the sashing rows. The quilt top should now measure 38" square.

4 Measure the quilt top through the center from side to side and trim two olive green 1 strips to this measurement. Sew the strips to the top and bottom edges of the quilt top. Press the seam allowances toward the borders. Measure the quilt top through the center from top to bottom, including the borders, and cut the remaining two olive green 1 strips to this measurement. Sew the strips to the sides of the quilt top. Press the seam allowances toward the borders.

5 Repeat step 4 with the large-scale floral 8"-wide strips, trimming the 42"-long strips to fit the top and bottom edges and the 58"-long strips to fit the sides.

FINISHING THE QUILT

1 Prepare a quilt backing that is 6" longer and wider than the quilt top.

2 Layer the backing, batting, and quilt top. Pin, hand baste, or spray baste the layers together.

3 Quilt using your preferred method. Trim the excess batting and backing even with the edges of the quilt top.

4 Using the pink-and-navy strips, make and attach the binding, referring to page 10 as needed.

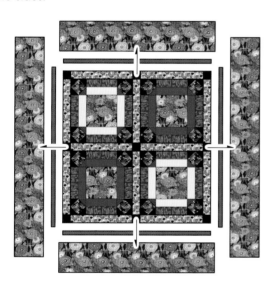

Quilt assembly

THE *Comfort* QUILT

This large block is straight out of the Depression era of the 1930s. It first appeared in the *Kansas City Star* newspaper as one of the series blocks released on a weekly basis. The original block was supersized to accommodate the large-scale print.

Block Finished Size: 18" x 18" ■ Number of Blocks in Quilt: 16 ■ Quilt Finished Size: 95" x 95"

MATERIALS

Yardages are based on 42"-wide fabrics.

3 yards of large-scale orange-and-turquoise floral for border

2⅛ yards of brown-and-turquoise print for blocks and sashing

2 yards of large-scale orange print for blocks

1⅞ yards of yellow feather print for blocks, sashing squares, and binding

1⅜ yards of large-scale green-and-turquoise print for blocks

⅔ yard of brown-and-cream dot print for blocks and sashing squares

9½ yards of fabric for backing

103" x 103" square of batting

CUTTING

From the brown-and-turquoise print, cut:

8 strips, 2½" x 42"; crosscut into 64 rectangles, 2½" x 4½"

20 strips, 2½" x 42"; crosscut into 40 strips, 2½" x 18½"

From the large-scale orange print for blocks, cut:

4 strips, 4½" x 42"; crosscut into 32 squares, 4½" x 4½"

1 strip, 2½" x 42"; crosscut into 8 squares, 2½" x 2½"

4 strips, 10½" x 42"; crosscut into 32 rectangles, 4½" x 10½"

From the large-scale green-and-turquoise print, cut:

1 strip, 2½" x 42"; crosscut into 8 squares, 2½" x 2½"

4 strips, 10½" x 42"; crosscut into 32 rectangles, 4½" x 10½"

From the yellow feather print, cut:

8 strips, 4½" x 42"; crosscut into 64 squares, 4½" x 4½"

1 strip, 2½" x 42"; crosscut into 9 squares, 2½" x 2½"

10 strips, 2⅛" x 42"

From the brown-and-cream dot print, cut:

4 strips, 4½" x 42"; crosscut into 32 squares, 4½" x 4½"

1 strip, 2½" x 42"; crosscut into 16 squares, 2½" x 2½"

From the *lengthwise grain* of the large-scale orange-and-turquoise floral, cut:

2 strips, 7" x 83"

2 strips, 7" x 97"

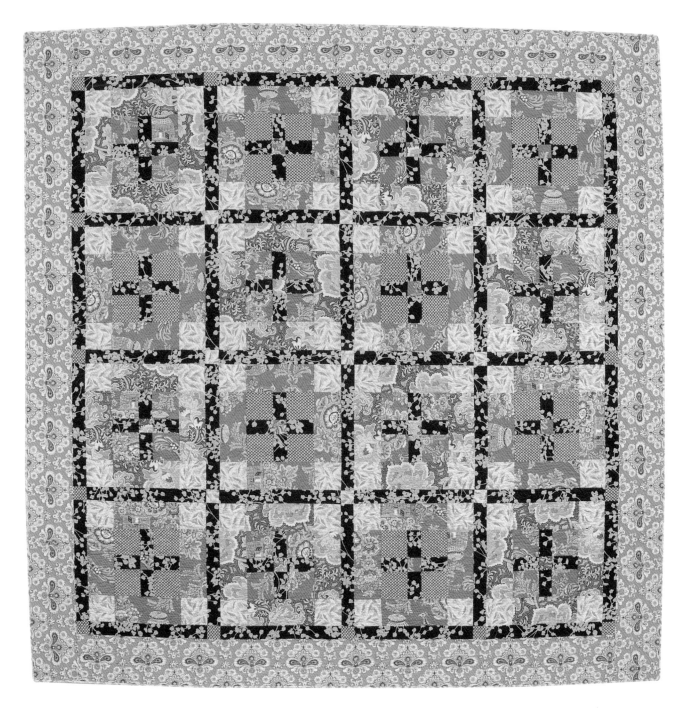

Designed and sewn by Jean Ann Wright; machine quilted by Shannon Baker.

MAKING THE BLOCKS

You will be making two color variations of the same block.

1. To make block A, sew a brown-and-turquoise rectangle between two orange print 4½" squares. Press the seam allowances toward the rectangle. Repeat to make a total of 16 units.

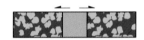

Make 16.

2. Sew a green-and-turquoise square between two brown-and-turquoise rectangles. Press the seam allowances toward the rectangles. Repeat to make a total of eight units.

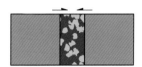

Make 8.

3. Sew a unit from step 2 between two units from step 1 to make a center unit. Press the seam allowances toward the units from step 2. Repeat to make a total of eight units.

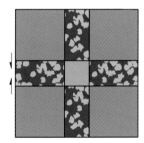

Make 8.

4. Sew a green-and-turquoise rectangle to two opposite sides of a center unit. Press the seam allowances toward the rectangles. Add a yellow 4½" square to the ends of two additional green-and-turquoise rectangles. Press the seam allowances toward the rectangles. Join these strips to the

remaining edges of the block center to complete block A. Press the seam allowances toward the newly added strips. Repeat to make a total of eight blocks measuring 18½" square.

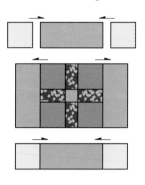
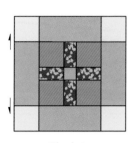

Block A.
Make 8.

5. To make block B, refer to steps 1–3 to sew the brown-and-turquoise rectangles, the brown-and-cream 4½" squares, and the orange print 2½" squares together to make eight center units.

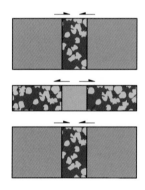
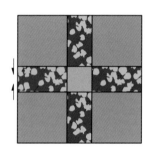

Make 8.

6. Refer to step 4 to complete the blocks, using the orange print rectangles and yellow 4½" squares.

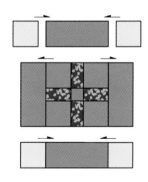
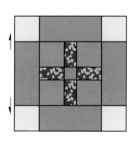

Block B.
Make 8.

ASSEMBLING THE QUILT TOP

1 Alternately sew two each of blocks A and B together with five brown-and-turquoise sashing strips as shown to make two each of block rows A and B. Press the seam allowances toward the sashing strips.

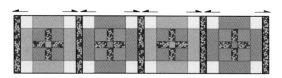

Row A.
Make 2.

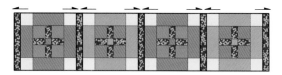

Row B.
Make 2.

2 Alternately join five brown-and-cream 2½" squares and four brown-and-turquoise strips to make the top sashing row. Press the seam allowances toward the strips. Repeat to make the bottom sashing row.

Top/bottom sashing.
Make 2.

3 Join two brown-and-cream 2½" squares, three yellow 2½" squares, and four brown-and-turquoise strips as shown to make a center sashing row. Press the seam allowances toward the strips. Repeat to make a total of three center sashing rows.

Center sashing.
Make 3.

4 Refer to the quilt assembly diagram to join the sashing rows and block rows, being careful to alternate the block rows and to position the sashing rows correctly. Press the seam allowances toward the sashing rows. The quilt top should now measure 82½" x 82½".

5 Measure the quilt top through the center from side to side. Trim two orange-and-turquoise 7" x 83" strips to this measurement. Sew the strips to the top and bottom edges of the quilt top. Press the seam allowances toward the borders. Measure the quilt top through the center from top to bottom, including the borders, and cut the remaining two orange-and-turquoise strips to this measurement. Sew the strips to the sides of the quilt top. Press the seam allowances toward the borders.

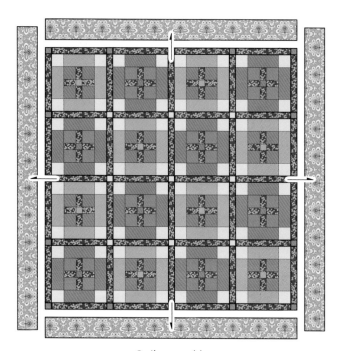

Quilt assembly

FINISHING THE QUILT

1 Prepare a quilt backing that is 6" longer and wider than the quilt top.

2 Layer the backing, batting, and quilt top. Pin, hand baste, or spray baste the layers together.

3 Quilt using your preferred method. Trim the excess batting and backing even with the edges of the quilt top.

4 Using the yellow strips, make and attach the binding, referring to page 10 as needed.

GOOD-LUCK *Pansies*

This quilt includes a lot of floral prints, but the deep, rich colors keep them from being too sweet, and the alternating light prints give the entire quilt extra depth. Don't let the mitered angles in the block scare you off; they're easy to accomplish with your rotary cutter and a little magic!

Block Finished Size: 13¼" x 13¼" ■ Number of Blocks in Quilt: 16 ■ Quilt Finished Size: 79" x 79"

MATERIALS

Yardages are based on 42"-wide fabrics.

2⅞ yards of red striped fabric for sashing and binding

2½ yards of large-scale pansy border print for border

⅝ yard of pink small-scale pansy print with light background for blocks and sashing squares

⅓ yard *each* of 7 assorted light prints

⅓ yard *each* of 8 assorted dark prints

5 yards of fabric for backing

85" x 85" square of batting

CUTTING

From *each* of the 7 assorted light prints, cut:
2 strips, 4" x 42" (14 total)

From *each* of the 8 assorted dark prints, cut:
2 strips, 4" x 42" (16 total)

From the pink small-scale pansy print, cut:
2 strips, 4" x 42"
3 strips, 3½" x 42"; crosscut into 25 squares, 3½" x 3½"

From the red striped fabric, cut:
20 strips, 3½" x 42"; crosscut into 40 strips, 3½" x 13¾"
9 strips, 2⅛" x 42"

From the *lengthwise grain* of the large-scale pansy border print, cut:
4 strips, 6" x 82"

Designed and sewn by Debby Kratovil; machine quilted by Cathy MacDonald.

MAKING THE BLOCKS

1 Sew a light strip to a dark strip along the long edges to make a strip set. Press the seam allowance toward the dark strip. Repeat to make one additional strip set from the same two fabrics. Repeat with the remaining light and dark strips, including the two small-scale pansy strips in the light assortment, to make a total of eight matching pairs of strip sets. Crosscut each pair of strip sets into eight 7½"-wide segments (64 total).

Make 8 pairs of matching strip sets (16 total).
Cut 8 segments from each pair (64 total).

2 Place two matching segments face up and side by side. Cut the segment on the left in half diagonally from the lower-right corner to the upper-left corner. Cut the segment on the right in half diagonally from the lower-left corner to the upper-right corner. Mark the pieces A, B, C, and D as shown. Cut and mark the remaining six matching segments in the same manner, keeping like triangles together. Repeat with the segments from each of the remaining strip sets.

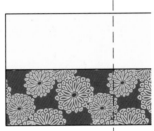

3 Working with matching pieces, sew each A triangle to a D triangle to make unit 1. Sew each B triangle to a C triangle to make unit 2. Make a total of four unit 1 squares and four unit 2 squares from *each* fabric combination. The units should measure 7⅛" square.

Unit 1.
Make 4 of each
fabric combination.

Unit 2.
Make 4 of each
fabric combination.

4 Sew four matching unit 1 squares together as shown to make block 1. Sew four matching unit 2 squares together as shown to make block 2. Repeat to make a total of eight block 1 and eight block 2 measuring 13¾" square.

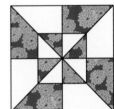

Make 8 of each.

ASSEMBLING THE QUILT TOP

1. Alternately join five red striped 3½" x 13¾" sashing strips and four different blocks to make a block row. Press the seam allowances toward the sashing strips. Repeat to make a total of four rows. It doesn't matter what combination of block 1 and block 2 you use in each row, but you may want to arrange the blocks into four rows of four blocks each on a design wall to find a pleasing arrangement before you sew the rows together.

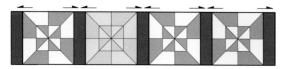

Make 4.

2. Alternately sew five pansy squares and four red striped 3½" x 13¾" strips together to make a sashing row. Press the seam allowances toward the strips. Repeat to make a total of five sashing rows.

Make 5.

3. Refer to the quilt assembly diagram to alternately sew the sashing rows and block rows together. Press the seam allowances toward the sashing rows. The quilt top should now measure 68½" square.

4. Refer to "Magical Mitered Corners" on page 10 to add the pansy 6"-wide border strips to the quilt top.

Quilt assembly

FINISHING THE QUILT

1. Prepare a quilt backing that is 6" longer and wider than the quilt top.

2. Layer the backing, batting, and quilt top. Pin, hand baste, or spray baste the layers together.

3. Quilt using your preferred method. Trim the excess batting and backing even with the edges of the quilt top.

4. Using the red striped 2⅛"-wide strips, make and attach the binding, referring to page 10 as needed.

Texas STARS

Nine stars in three variations make up this patriotic American beauty. The star blocks are quick to make with rotary-cutting techniques, and there are no set-in seams! I used a large variety of red and blue prints to lend interest to this quilt, which also makes it perfect for digging into your own patriotic stash.

Block Finished Size: 19½" x 19½" ■ Number of Blocks in Quilt: 9 ■ Quilt Finished Size: 89½" x 89½"

MATERIALS

Yardages are based on 42"-wide fabrics.

3½ yards of red bandana print for border and binding

⅜ yard *each* of 9 assorted light prints for block backgrounds

⅓ yard *each* of 7 to 9 assorted red prints for block stars

⅓ yard *each* of 7 to 9 assorted blue prints for block stars

1¼ yards of red striped fabric for sashing

⅝ yard of navy blue print for inner border

¼ yard of medium blue print for sashing squares

8¼ yards of fabric for backing

98" x 98" square of batting

CUTTING

From the 7 to 9 assorted red prints, cut a *total* of:
3 strips, 4½" x 42"

10 strips, 2½" x 42" (cut at least 2 strips from each of 3 fabrics)

From the 7 to 9 assorted blue prints, cut a *total* of:
5 strips, 4½" x 42"

10 strips, 2½" x 42" (cut at least 2 strips from each of 3 fabrics)

From *each* of the 9 assorted light prints, cut:
4 squares, 6⅝" x 6⅝"; cut each square once diagonally to yield 8 triangles

4 squares, 4⅞" x 4⅞"; cut each square once diagonally to yield 8 triangles

From the red striped fabric, cut:
24 strips, 3½" x 20"

From the medium blue print, cut:
2 strips, 3½" x 42"; crosscut into 16 squares, 3½" x 3½"

From the navy blue print, cut:
8 strips, 2" x 42"

From the red bandana print, cut:
10 strips, 2⅛" x 42"

From the *lengthwise grain* of the remaining red bandana print, cut:
4 strips, 8½" x length of fabric

Designed and sewn by Debby Kratovil; machine quilted by Cathy MacDonald.

MAKING THE DIAMONDS

The quilt consists of three different blocks, but the arrangement of the whole diamonds and four-patch diamonds creates many different looks. Refer to the quilt photo and the block diagrams to help you with the arrangement to make each block unique.

Whole diamonds are cut from a strip of fabric, and four-patch diamonds are created by cutting segments from a strip set. Refer to the following instructions when making each block to cut the specific diamond shapes.

Whole Diamonds

1. Trim the right-hand end of a blue or red 4½"-wide strip at a 45° angle. To do this, line up the 45° line on your ruler along the bottom edge of the strip; cut off the end and discard it.

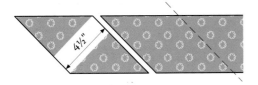

45° line

2. Rotate the strip so the angled end is on your left. Measure 4½" from the angled end and make another cut to create the diamond. Continue cutting from the angled edge until you have the required amount of diamonds.

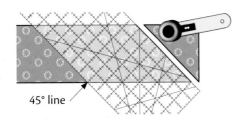

4½"

Four-Patch Diamonds

1. Stitch one red and one blue 2½"-wide strip together along the long edges, offsetting the strips 2½". Refer to step 1 of "Whole Diamonds" to trim one end of the strip set and then cut 2½"-wide segments, measuring from the angled end.

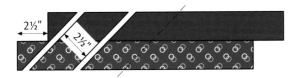

2½" 2½"

2. Sew two segments together as shown to make a four-patch diamond.

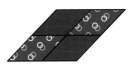

MAKING BLOCK 1

1. Select one red and one blue 4½"-wide strip. Refer to "Whole Diamonds" at left to cut four diamonds from each strip.

2. Sew a matching large and small light triangle to opposite sides of each diamond as shown. Press the seam allowances toward the triangles.

Make 4 of each.

3. Using the units from step 2, sew a blue unit to each red unit along the long edges as shown to make a quarter unit. Press the seam allowances open. The units should measure 10¼" square.

Make 4.

4. Arrange the quarter units into two rows of two units each so that the colors alternate. Sew the units in each row together. Press the seam allowances open. Sew the rows together. Press the seam allowances open. The block should measure 20" square.

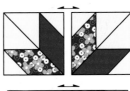 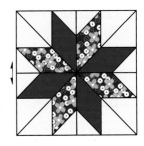

Block 1

⑤ Repeat steps 1–4 using different fabrics to make a total of two block 1.

MAKING BLOCK 2

① Select one pair of matching red and one pair of matching blue 2½"-wide strips. Refer to "Four-Patch Diamonds" on page 54 to sew one red and one blue strip together to make a strip set. Make two matching strip sets. Cut 16 segments from the strip sets and sew them together in pairs with the blue fabric at the points of the diamonds.

② Sew a matching large and small light triangle to opposite sides of each four-patch diamond as shown. Press the seam allowances toward the triangles.

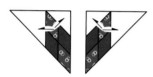

Make 4 of each.

③ Sew two units from step 2 together along the long edges as shown to make a quarter unit. Press the seam allowances open. The units should measure 10¼" square.

Make 4.

④ Arrange the quarter units into two rows of two units each as shown. Sew the units in each row together. Press the seam allowances open. Sew the rows together. Press the seam allowances open. The block should measure 20" square.

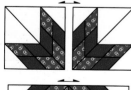
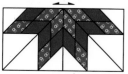
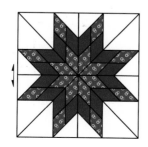

Block 3

⑤ Repeat steps 1–4 to make two additional block 2 as shown. Be careful to orient the segments for the four-patch diamonds so the diamond point is the correct color, noting that two different colorations of four-patch diamonds are used for one of the blocks.

Make 1 of each.

MAKING BLOCK 3

① Refer to "Whole Diamonds" on page 54 to cut four diamonds from one blue 4½"-wide strip.

② Select one red and one blue 2½"-wide strip. Refer to "Four-Patch Diamonds" on page 54 to sew them together and cut eight segments from the strip set. Sew the segments together in pairs so the red fabric is at the points of the diamonds.

③ Sew a matching large and small light triangle to opposite sides of each whole and four-patch diamond as shown. Press the seam allowances toward the triangles.

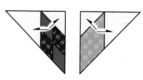

Make 4 of each.

④ Sew a whole-diamond unit to each four-patch-diamond unit along the long edges as shown to make a quarter unit. Press the seam allowances open. The units should measure 10¼" square.

Make 4.

5 Arrange the quarter units into two rows of two units each so that the whole and four-patch diamonds alternate. Sew the units in each row together. Press the seam allowances open. Sew the rows together. Press the seam allowances open. The block should measure 20" square.

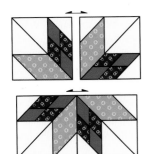
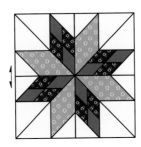

Block 2

6 Repeat steps 1–5 using the color combinations shown to make three additional block 3 as shown. Be careful to orient the segments for the four-patch diamonds as shown so the diamond point is the correct color.

Make 1 of each.

ASSEMBLING THE QUILT TOP

1 Using a design wall, arrange the blocks into three rows of three blocks each. Once you have determined the arrangement, alternately join four red striped sashing strips with the blocks in each row. Press the seam allowances toward the strips.

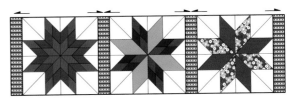

Make 3.

2 Alternately join four medium blue squares and three red striped sashing strips to make a sashing row. Press the seam allowances toward the strips. Repeat to make a total of four rows.

Make 4.

3 Refer to the quilt assembly diagram to alternately join the sashing and block rows. Press the seam allowances toward the sashing rows. The quilt top should now measure 71" square.

4 Sew two navy strips together end to end to make one long strip. Repeat to make a total of four pieced strips. Measure the quilt top through the center from top to bottom. Trim two of the pieced strips to this measurement and sew the strips to the sides of the quilt top. Press the seam allowances toward the borders. Measure the quilt top through the center from side to side, including the borders, and cut the remaining two pieced strips to this measurement. Sew the strips to the top and bottom edges of the quilt top. Press the seam allowances toward the borders. The quilt top should now measure 74" square.

5 Measure the quilt top through the center from top to bottom and trim two of the red bandana 8½"-wide strips to this measurement. Sew the strips to the sides of the quilt top. Press the seam allowances toward the borders. Measure the quilt top through the center from side to side, including the borders, and cut the remaining two red bandana strips to this measurement. Sew the strips to the top and bottom edges of the quilt top. Press the seam allowances toward the borders.

FINISHING THE QUILT

1 Prepare a quilt backing that is 6" longer and wider than the quilt top.

2 Layer the backing, batting, and quilt top. Pin, hand baste, or spray baste the layers together.

3 Quilt using your preferred method. Trim the excess batting and backing even with the edges of the quilt top.

4 Using the red bandana 2⅛"-wide strips, make and attach the binding, referring to page 10 as needed.

Quilt assembly

IT'S EASY BEING *Green*

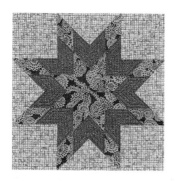

This is my quilting contribution to being environmentally green. One large star dressed up in lush green blooms makes for a quick project for a child's quilt or something to grace your wall. Rotary cutting the diamonds and triangles is truly easy.

Block Finished Size: 29" x 29" ■ Number of Blocks in Quilt: 1 ■ Quilt Finished Size: 41" x 41"

MATERIALS

Yardages are based on 42"-wide fabrics.

1½ yards of large-scale green directional print for border (or ¾ yard of nondirectional print)

1 yard of purple print for star, inner border, and binding

⅝ yard of light green print for block background

⅜ yard of large-scale green floral for star

2⅞ yards of fabric for backing

47" x 47" square of batting

CUTTING

Because you'll be working with bias edges on both the diamonds and triangles, it's very helpful to prepare the fabric with spray starch or sizing before you cut the pieces. The extra stiffness helps eliminate stretching and distortion.

From the large-scale green floral, cut:
3 strips, 3½" x 42"

From the purple print, cut:
3 strips, 3½" x 42"
4 strips, 1½" x 42"
5 strips, 2⅛" x 42"

From the light green print, cut:
4 squares, 9⅝" x 9⅝"; cut once diagonally to yield 8 large triangles
4 squares, 6¾" x 6¾"; cut once diagonally to yield 8 small triangles

From the large-scale green directional print for border, cut:
2 strips, 5½" x 32"
2 strips, 5½" x 42"

Designed and sewn by Debby Kratovil; machine quilted by Cathy MacDonald.

MAKING THE BLOCK

1 Sew a green floral strip to a purple 3½" x 42" strip to make a strip set, offsetting one strip 3" as shown. Press the seam allowance toward the green strip. Repeat to make a total of three strip sets.

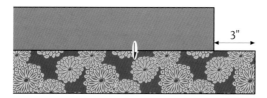

Make 3 strip sets.

2 Trim the right-hand end of each strip set at a 45° angle. To do this, line up the 45° line on your ruler along the bottom edge of the strip; cut off the end and discard it. Rotate the strip so the angled end is on your left. Measuring from the angled end, cut 16 segments, 3½" wide.

Cut 16 segments.

3 Sew two segments together as shown. Repeat to make a total of eight four-patch diamonds.

Make 8.

4 Sew a large and small light green triangle to opposite sides of each diamond as shown. Press the seam allowances toward the triangles. Make four of each unit.

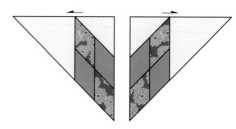

Make 4 of each.

5 Sew two units from step 4 together along the long edges as shown to make a quarter unit. Press the seam allowances open. The units should measure 15" square.

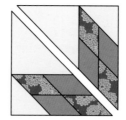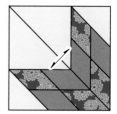

Make 4.

ASSEMBLING THE QUILT TOP

1 Refer to the quilt assembly diagram to arrange the quarter units into two rows of two units each. Sew the units in each row together. Press the seam allowances open. Sew the rows together. Press the seam allowances open. The block should measure 29½" square.

2 Measure the quilt top from side to side and trim two of the purple 1½" x 42" strips to this measurement. Sew the strips to the top and bottom edges of the quilt top. Press the seam allowances toward the borders. Measure the quilt top from top to bottom, including the borders, and trim the remaining two purple strips to this measurement. Sew the strips to the sides of the quilt top. Press the seam allowances toward the borders.

3 Repeat step 2 with the green border-print strips to add the outer borders, trimming the 32"-long strips to fit the top and bottom edges and the 42"-long strips to fit the sides.

Quilt assembly

FINISHING THE QUILT

1 Prepare a quilt backing that is 6" longer and wider than the quilt top.

2 Layer the backing, batting, and quilt top. Pin, hand baste, or spray baste the layers together.

3 Quilt using your preferred method. Trim the excess batting and backing even with the edges of the quilt top.

4 Using the purple 2⅛"-wide strips, make and attach the binding, referring to page 10 as needed.

Facets OF COLOR QUILT

The deep, rich colors in this quilt remind me of rare gems that are cut in such a way that each facet captures the light and radiates in all its splendor. Fabric is much cheaper than rare gems! I used my rotary cutter to slice and reveal all the beauty of these color-drenched fabrics. On page 68, you can make a table runner using the same paper-pieced block in a different colorway.

Block Finished Size: 18" x 18" ■ Number of Blocks in Quilt: 4 ■ Quilt Finished Size: 64" x 64"

MATERIALS

Yardages are based on 42"-wide fabrics.

2½ yards of blue print 1 for outer border and binding

1⅛ yards of blue print 2 for blocks

1 yard of blue print 3 for blocks and sashing strips

¾ yard of lavender print for blocks and sashing squares

⅔ yard of lime green print for block backgrounds

½ yard of red striped fabric for inner border

¼ yard of red print for blocks

4 yards of fabric for backing

69" x 69" square of batting

Foundation paper

CUTTING

From the blue print 2, cut:

4 strips, 7" x 42"; crosscut into 16 squares, 7" x 7"

1 strip, 4¾" x 42"; crosscut into 4 squares, 4¾" x 4¾"

From the lime green print, cut:

1 strip, 4½" x 42"; crosscut into 8 squares, 4½" x 4½". Cut each square once diagonally to yield 16 half-square triangles.

2 strips, 7½" x 42"; crosscut into 16 rectangles, 5" x 7½". Stack 8 rectangles right side up and 8 rectangles wrong side up and cut once diagonally in the same direction to yield 32 half-rectangle triangles.

From the lavender print, cut:

1 strip, 3⅞" x 42"; crosscut into 8 squares, 3⅞" x 3⅞". Cut each square once diagonally to yield 16 half-square triangles.

2 strips, 7¼" x 7¼"; crosscut into 8 squares, 7¼" x 7¼". Cut each square twice diagonally to yield 32 quarter-square triangles.

1 strip, 3½" x 42"; crosscut into 9 squares, 3½" x 3½"

Designed and sewn by Debby Kratovil; machine quilted by Leslie Evans.

From the red print, cut:

1 strip, 7¼" x 42"; crosscut into 4 squares, 7¼" x 7¼". Cut each square twice diagonally to yield 16 quarter-square triangles.

From the blue print 3, cut:

6 strips, 3½" x 42"; crosscut into 12 strips, 3½" x 18½"

1 strip, 7¼" x 42"; crosscut into 4 squares, 7¼" x 7¼". Cut each square twice diagonally to yield 16 quarter-square triangles.

From the red striped fabric, cut:

5 strips, 2½" x 42"

From the blue print 1, cut:

8 strips, 2⅛" x 42"

From the *lengthwise grain* of the remaining blue print 1, cut:

4 strips, 8" x length of fabric

MAKING THE BLOCKS

1 Refer to "Paper Piecing" on page 7 to make 16 copies of the block-corner unit on page 67 using your preferred method. Paper piece each unit, using the 7" blue print 2 squares for area 1, the lime green half-rectangle triangles for areas 2 and 3, and the lime green half-square triangles for area 4. Trim away any excess fabric extending beyond the outer line of each unit. Remove the paper foundations.

Make 16.

2 Sew a lavender half-square triangle to opposite sides of a 4¾" blue print 2 square. Press the seam allowances toward the triangles. Add a triangle to the remaining two sides of the square to complete

the square-in-a-square unit. Repeat to make a total of four units for the block centers.

Make 4.

3 Sew each red and blue print 3 quarter-square triangle to a lavender quarter-square triangle along the short edges. Press the seam allowance toward the red and blue triangles. Sew a red-and-lavender pieced triangle to a blue-and-lavender pieced triangle to make an hourglass unit. Press the seam allowance open. Repeat to make a total of 16 hourglass units.

Make 16.

4 Arrange four paper-pieced units, one square-in-a-square unit, and four hourglass units into three rows as shown. Sew the units in each row together. Press the seam allowances as indicated. Sew the rows together. Press the seam allowances toward the center row. Repeat to make a total of four blocks measuring 18½" square.

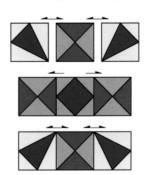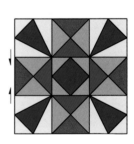

Make 4.

ASSEMBLING THE QUILT TOP

1 Alternately join three lavender squares and two blue print 3 sashing strips to make a sashing row. Press the seam allowances toward the strips. Repeat to make a total of three rows.

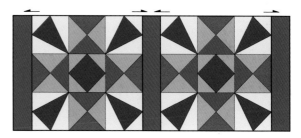

Make 3.

2 Alternately join three blue print 3 sashing strips and two blocks to make a block row. Press the seam allowances toward the strips. Repeat to make a total of two rows.

Make 2.

3 Refer to the quilt assembly diagram to alternately sew the sashing rows and block rows together. Press the seam allowances toward the sashing rows. The quilt top should measure 45½" square.

4 Sew the red striped strips together end to end to make one long strip. Measure the quilt top through the center from top to bottom. From the pieced strip, cut two strips to this measurement and sew them to the sides of the quilt top. Press the seam allowances toward the borders. Measure the quilt top from side to side, including the border. From the remainder of the pieced strip, cut two strips to this measurement and sew them to the top and bottom edges of the quilt top. Press the seam allowances toward the borders. The quilt top should now measure 49½" square.

5 Measure the quilt top through the center from side to side and trim two of the 8"-wide blue print 1 strips to this measurement. Sew the strips to the top and bottom edges of the quilt top. Press the seam allowances toward the borders. Measure the quilt top through the center from top to bottom, including the borders, and cut the remaining two blue print 1 strips to this measurement. Sew the strips to the sides of the quilt top. Press the seam allowances toward the borders.

FINISHING THE QUILT

1 Prepare a quilt backing that is 6" longer and wider than the quilt top.

2 Layer the backing, batting, and quilt top. Pin, hand baste, or spray baste the layers together.

3 Quilt using your preferred method. Trim the excess batting and backing even with the edges of the quilt top.

4 Using the 2⅛"-wide blue print 1 strips, make and attach the binding, referring to page 10 as needed.

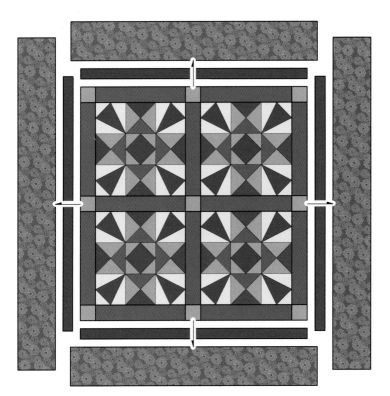

Quilt assembly

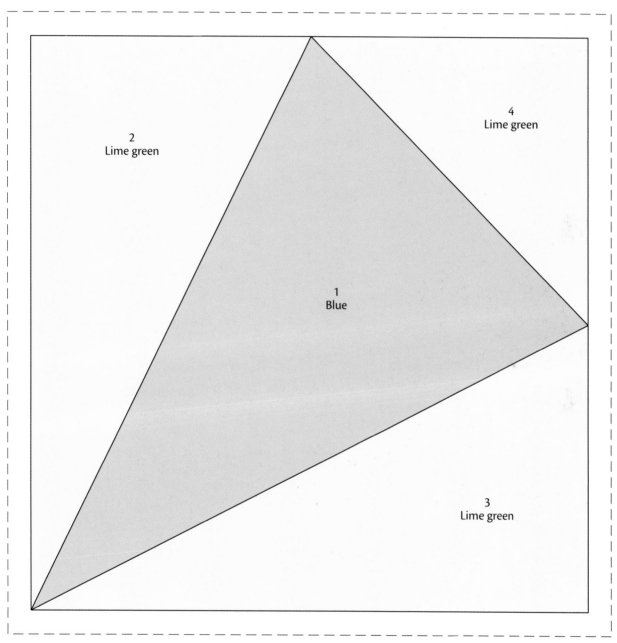

2
Lime green

4
Lime green

1
Blue

3
Lime green

Corner unit

Facets OF COLOR TABLE RUNNER

I designed this table runner as a teaching project so that I could introduce my students to a variety of quilting techniques and triangle formulas. Conquering the triangle with paper-piecing techniques gives the average quilter the confidence to work with a larger variety of quilt blocks. I love the "aha!" moment when points are sharp and seams match!

Block Finished Size: 18" x 18" ■ Number of Blocks in Table Runner: 2 ■ Table Runner Finished Size: 29" x 49"

MATERIALS

Yardages are based on 42"-wide fabrics.

1⅜ yards of brown circle print for border and binding

1 yard of black floral for blocks and sashing strips

⅝ yard of light orange speckled print for blocks and sashing squares

¼ yard of dark orange solid for blocks

1 fat eighth of black ribbon print for blocks

1⅝ yards of fabric for backing

35" x 55" piece of batting

Foundation paper

CUTTING

From the black floral, cut:

4 strips, 2½" x 42"; crosscut into 7 strips, 2½" x 18½"

4 squares, 7¼" x 7¼"; cut twice diagonally to yield 16 quarter-square triangles

2 strips, 7" x 42"; crosscut into 8 squares, 7" x 7"

From the light orange speckled print, cut:

2 squares, 7¼" x 7¼"; cut twice diagonally to yield 8 quarter-square triangles

4 squares, 4½" x 4½"; cut once diagonally to yield 8 half-square triangles

1 strip, 2½" x 42"; crosscut into 6 squares, 2½" x 2½"

1 strip, 7½" x 42"; crosscut into 8 rectangles, 5" x 7½". Stack 4 rectangles right side up and 4 rectangles right side down and cut once diagonally in the same direction to yield 16 half-rectangles.

From the black ribbon print, cut:

2 squares, 4¾" x 4¾"

From the dark orange solid, cut:

2 squares, 7¼" x 7¼"; cut twice diagonally to yield 8 quarter-square triangles

4 squares, 3⅞" x 3⅞"; cut once diagonally to yield 8 half-square triangles

From the *lengthwise grain* of the brown circle print, cut:

2 strips, 4" x 45"

2 strips, 4" x 32"

4 strips, 2⅛" x length of fabric

Designed and sewn by Debby Kratovil.

MAKING THE BLOCKS

① Refer to "Paper Piecing" on page 7 to make 8 copies of the block-corner unit on page 67 using your preferred method. Paper piece each unit, using the black floral squares for area 1, the light orange half-rectangle triangles for areas 2 and 3, and the light orange half-square triangles for area 4. Trim away any excess fabric extending beyond the outer lines of each unit. Remove the paper foundations.

Make 8.

② Sew a dark orange half-square triangle to opposite sides of a ribbon-print square. Press the seam allowances toward the triangles. Add a triangle to the remaining two sides of the square to complete the square-in-a-square unit. Repeat to make a total of two units for the block centers.

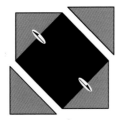

Make 2.

③ Sew each dark orange and light orange quarter-square triangle to a black floral quarter-square triangle along the short edges. Press the seam allowances toward the dark orange and light orange triangles. Sew a black/dark orange pieced triangle to a black/light orange pieced triangle to make an

hourglass unit. Press the seam allowances open. Repeat to make a total of eight hourglass units.

Make 8.

④ Arrange four paper-pieced units, one square-in-a-square unit, and four hourglass units into three rows as shown. Sew the units in each row together. Press the seam allowances as indicated. Sew the rows together. Press the seam allowances toward the center row. Repeat to make a total of two blocks measuring 18½" square.

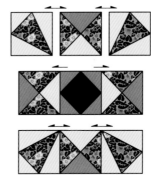 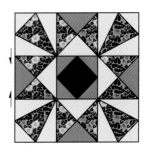

Make 2.

ASSEMBLING THE TABLE-RUNNER TOP

① Alternately join two light orange squares and one black floral 2½" x 18½" sashing strip to make a sashing row. Press the seam allowances toward the strip. Repeat to make a total of three rows.

Make 3.

2 Alternately join two black floral sashing strips and one block to make a block row. Press the seam allowances toward the strips. Repeat to make a total of two block rows.

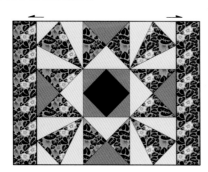

Make 2.

3 Refer to the table runner assembly diagram to alternately sew the sashing rows and block rows together. Press the seam allowances toward the sashing rows. The table runner should measure 22½" x 42½".

4 Measure the table-runner top from top to bottom and trim the brown 4" x 45" strips to this measurement. Sew the strips to the sides of the table-runner top. Press the seam allowances toward the border. Measure the table-runner top from side to side, including the borders, and trim the brown 4" x 32" strips to this measurement. Sew the strips to the top and bottom edges of the table-runner top. Press the seam allowances toward the border.

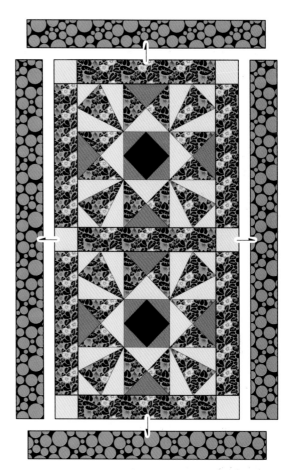

Table runner assembly

FINISHING THE TABLE RUNNER

1 Prepare a backing that is 6" longer and wider than the quilt top.

2 Layer the backing, batting, and quilt top. Pin, hand baste, or spray baste the layers together.

3 Quilt, using your preferred method. Trim the excess batting and backing even with the edges of the table-runner top.

4 Using the brown 2⅛"-wide strips, make and attach the binding, referring to page 10 as needed.

THAT *Spikey* THING

The inspiration for this quilt came from a photograph of a folk-art quilt from the early 1930s. Huge appliqué blocks were surrounded with elongated triangles. I drafted my own pattern and selected a large-scale floral print as the focus, pulling fabrics that read as solids for the spikes. Paper piecing these spikes ensures very, very sharp points.

Block Finished Size: 21" x 21" ■ Number of Blocks in Quilt: 4 ■ Quilt Finished Size: 68" x 68"

MATERIALS

Yardages are based on 42"-wide fabrics.

2⅛ yards of purple-and-green striped fabric for outer border

1⅓ yards of large-scale purple floral for blocks and sashing rectangles

1⅝ yards of light green dot print for block backgrounds

⅜ yard each of 4 assorted fabrics for star points and sashing squares

⅓ yard of dark yellow solid for inner border

⅝ yard of brown print for binding

4¼ yards of fabric for backing

75" x 75" square of batting

Foundation paper

CUTTING

From the large-scale purple floral, cut:

4 strips, 7½" x 42"; crosscut into 20 squares, 7½" x 7½"

3 strips, 3½" x 42"; crosscut into 12 rectangles, 3½" x 7½"

From the light green dot print, cut:

5 strips, 3½" x 42"; crosscut into 24 rectangles, 3½" x 7½"

7 strips, 2½" x 42"; crosscut into 32 rectangles, 2½" x 8"

4 strips, 4¼" x 42"; crosscut into 16 rectangles, 4¼" x 8"

From *each* of the 4 assorted prints, cut:

3 strips, 2½" x 42"; crosscut into:

8 rectangles, 2½" x 8"

8 rectangles, 2½" x 4¾"

From the remainder of the assorted prints, cut a *total* of:

9 squares, 3½" x 3½"

From the dark yellow, cut:

6 strips, 1½" x 42"

From the *lengthwise grain* of the purple-and-green striped fabric, cut:

4 strips, 8" x 70"

From the brown print, cut:

8 strips, 2⅛" x 42"

Designed and sewn by Debby Kratovil; machine quilted by Cathy MacDonald.

MAKING THE BLOCKS

① Refer to "Paper Piecing" on page 7 to make 16 copies of the block unit on page 75 using your preferred method. Paper piece each unit using the light green 4¼" x 8" rectangles for area 1, the assorted color 2½" x 8" rectangles for areas 2 and 3, the light green 2½" x 8" rectangles for areas 4 and 5, and the assorted color 2½" x 4¾" rectangles for areas 6 and 7. Be sure to use the same assorted color rectangles in each unit. Make four units of each assorted color spikes (16 total).Trim away any excess fabric extending beyond the outer line of each unit. Remove the paper foundations.

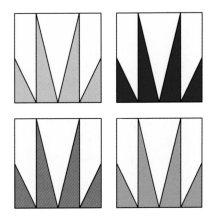

Make 4 of each color (16 total).

② Arrange four matching paper-pieced units and five purple floral squares into three rows as shown. Sew the squares in each row together. Press the seam allowances toward the purple squares. Sew the rows together. Press the seam allowances open. Repeat to make a total of four blocks measuring 21½" square.

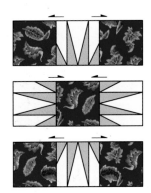
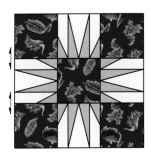

Make 4 (1 of each color).

ASSEMBLING THE QUILT TOP

① Alternately sew two light green 3½" x 7½" rectangles and one purple floral rectangle together. Press the seam allowances toward the purple rectangles. Repeat to make a total of six vertical pieced sashing strips.

Make 6.

② Alternately sew three pieced sashing strips and two blocks together. Press the seam allowances toward the strips. Repeat to make a total of two block rows.

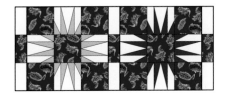

Make 2.

③ Sew three different assorted-color squares, four light green 3½" x 7½" rectangles, and two purple floral rectangles together as shown. Press the seam allowances away from the green rectangles. Repeat to make a total of three horizontal sashing rows.

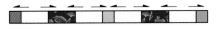

Make 3.

④ Refer to the photo on page 73 to alternately join the sashing rows and block rows. Press the seam allowances toward the sashing rows. The quilt top should measure 51½" x 51½".

⑤ Sew the dark yellow strips together end to end to make one long strip. Measure the quilt top from side to side. From the pieced strip, cut two strips to this measurement and sew them to the top and bottom edges of the quilt top. Press the seam allowances toward the borders. Measure the quilt top from top to bottom, including the border. From the remainder of the pieced strip, cut two strips to this measurement and sew them to the sides of the quilt top. Press the seam allowances toward the borders. The quilt top should now measure 53½" square.

6 Refer to "Magical Mitered Corners" on page 10 to add the purple-and-green striped 8"-wide border strips to the quilt top.

FINISHING THE QUILT

1 Prepare a backing that is 6" longer and wider than the quilt top.

2 Layer the backing, batting, and quilt top. Pin, hand baste, or spray baste the layers together.

3 Quilt using your preferred method. Trim the excess batting and backing even with the edges of the quilt top.

4 Using the brown strips, make and attach the binding, referring to page 10 as needed.

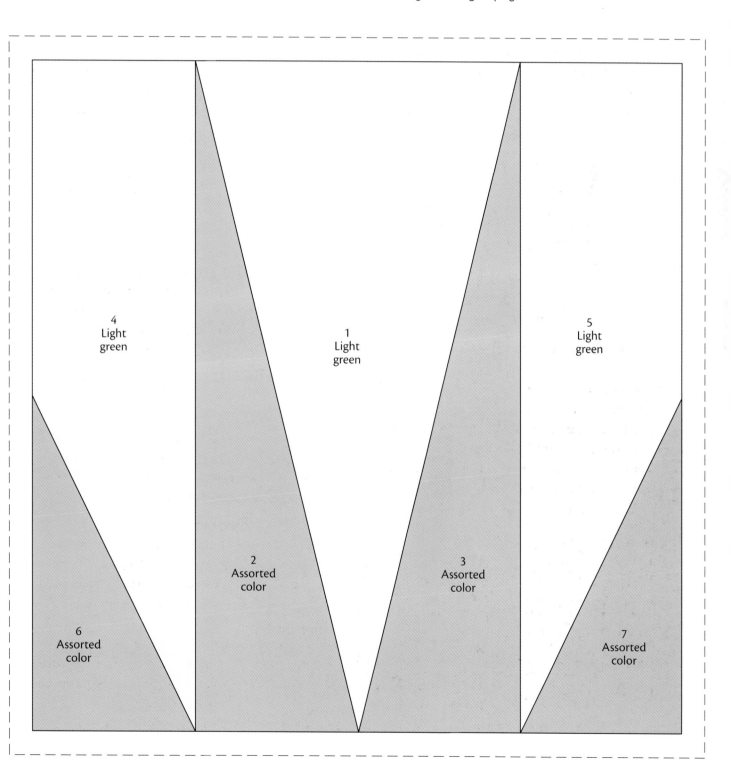

Secret GARDEN ALBUM

The Album block was a favorite of pioneers going west on wagon trains. Friends and family members could write a favorite sentiment or good wishes in the center bar of the block, making the quilt a scrapbook of memories for the departing families. Take a step back in time and make your own Album quilt using today's fabulous prints and easy techniques.

Block Finished Size: 16" x 16" ■ Number of Blocks in Quilt: 9 ■ Quilt Finished Size: 72" x 72"

MATERIALS

Yardages are based on 42"-wide fabrics.

2½ yards of cream print for block backgrounds, sashing, and border

½ yard *each* of 8 assorted prints for blocks and border

1 yard of red-and-blue floral for center block, corner squares, and binding

4½ yards of fabric for backing

76" x 76" square of batting

CUTTING

From *each* of 4 of the assorted prints, cut:

2 strips, 3⅜" x 42"; crosscut into:

    2 squares, 3⅜" x 3⅜" (A)

    2 rectangles, 3⅜" x 9" (B)

    6 rectangles, 3⅜" x 6⅛" (C)

1 strip, 8½" x 42"; crosscut into 2 rectangles, 8½" x 16½"

From *each* of the remaining 4 assorted prints, cut:

2 strips, 3⅜" x 42"; crosscut into:

    2 squares, 3⅜" x 3⅜" (A)

    2 rectangles, 3⅜" x 9" (B)

6 rectangles, 3⅜" x 6⅛" (C)

1 rectangle, 8½" x 20½"

From the red-and-blue floral, cut:

2 strips, 3⅜" x 42"; crosscut into:

    2 squares, 3⅜" x 3⅜" (A)

    2 rectangles, 3⅜" x 9" (B)

    6 rectangles, 3⅜" x 6⅛" (C)

1 strip, 8½" x 42"; crosscut into 4 squares, 8½" x 8½"

8 strips, 2⅛" x 42"

From the cream print, cut:

4 strips, 3⅜" x 42"; crosscut into:

    18 squares, 3⅜" x 3⅜" (A)

    9 rectangles, 3⅜" x 9" (B)

4 strips, 5¼" x 42"; crosscut into 27 squares, 5¼" x 5¼". Cut each square twice diagonally to yield 108 quarter-square triangles (D).

2 strips, 2⅞" x 42"; crosscut into 18 squares, 2⅞" x 2⅞". Cut each square once diagonally to yield 36 half-square triangles (E).

14 strips, 2½" x 42"; crosscut 8 strips into:

    12 strips, 2½" x 16½"

    8 rectangles, 2½" x 8½"

Designed and sewn by Jean Ann Wright; machine quilted by Shannon Baker.

MAKING THE BLOCKS

1 Arrange the A, B, and C pieces cut from one of the assorted color prints and the cream A, B, D, and E pieces into diagonal rows as shown. Sew the pieces in each row together. Press the seam allowances as indicated. Join the rows to complete the block. Press the seam allowances away from the center row.

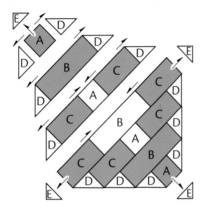

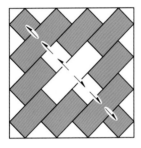

2 Repeat step 1 using the remaining assorted prints and the red-and-blue floral to make a total of nine blocks measuring 16½" square.

ASSEMBLING THE QUILT TOP

1 Arrange the blocks into three rows of three blocks each. Place the red-and-blue floral block in the center of the center row, and the four blocks with two matching 8½" x 16½" rectangles in each corner. Alternately join the blocks in each row with four cream 2½" x 16½" sashing strips. Press the seam allowances toward the strips.

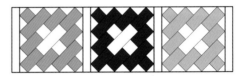

Make 3.

2 Sew the remaining six cream 2½" x 42" strips together end to end to make one long strip. Press the seam allowances in one direction. Measure the block rows from side to side. From the pieced strip, cut four strips to this measurement for the horizontal sashing rows. Refer to the quilt-assembly diagram to alternately join these strips with the block rows, using the arrangement you determined in step 1. Press the seam allowances toward the sashing rows.

3 Refer to the quilt-assembly diagram to arrange the 8½" x 16½" rectangles that match the blocks in each corner of the quilt top along the two adjacent outside edges. Place the 8½" x 20½" rectangles of the remaining assorted prints next to their matching block between these rectangles. To make the border strips, sew together the three rectangles on each of the four sides of the quilt top. Press the seam allowances away from the center rectangle. Add a cream 2½" x 8½" rectangle to the ends of each border strip. Press the seam allowances away from the cream rectangles. Sew the side borders to the sides of the quilt top. Press the seam allowances toward the borders. Join a red-and-blue 8½" square to the ends of the top and bottom borders. Press the seam allowances toward the squares.

Sew these borders to the top and bottom edges of the quilt top. Press the seam allowances toward the borders.

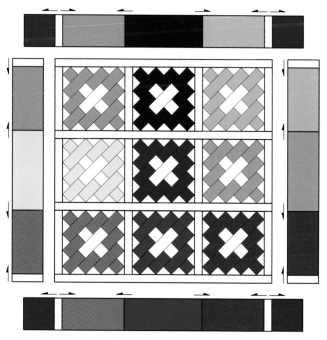

Quilt assembly

FINISHING THE QUILT

1. Prepare a backing that is 6" longer and wider than the quilt top.

2. Layer the backing, batting, and quilt top. Pin, hand baste, or spray baste the layers together.

3. Quilt using your preferred method. Trim the excess batting and backing even with the edges of the quilt top.

4. Using the red-and-blue strips, make and attach the binding, referring to page 10 as needed.

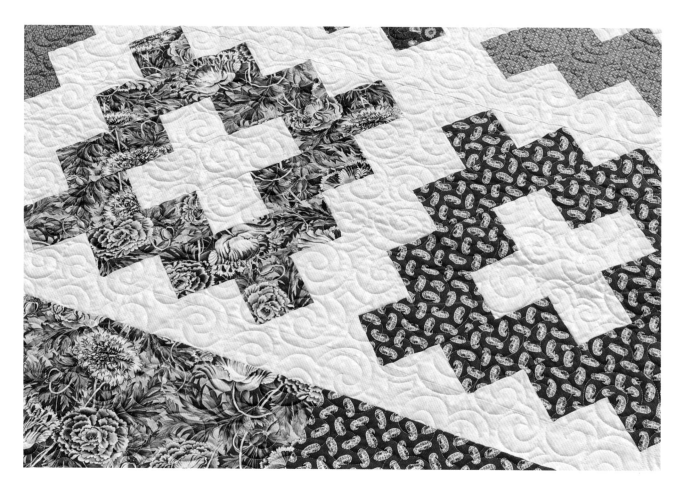

Modern GRACE

With just the simplest of fabrics you can create a graceful quilt that lets the fabrics do all the work. The pink flowers were cut from a companion print and then machine appliquéd to the top, turning otherwise tedious work into tremendous fun! If you can't find a fabric that will work for the cutouts, I've included a template for you to use with a similar colored fabric.

Block Finished Size: 25½" x 25½" ■ Number of Blocks in Quilt: 1 ■ Quilt Finished Size: 35½" x 35½"

MATERIALS

Yardages are based on 42"-wide fabrics.

⅝ yard of small-scale black-and-white floral for block

⅝ yard of pink-and-black print for block and outer border

½ yard of large-scale black-and-white floral for block

⅜ yard of black-and-white striped fabric for block and inner border

¼ yard of pink floral with motifs approximately 3½"-wide for appliqués or enough yardage to cut 8 motifs

⅓ yard of black-and-white print for binding

1⅛ yards of fabric for backing

40" x 40" square of batting

½ yard of 18"-wide paper-backed fusible web

Thread for machine appliqué

Freezer paper (needed only to cut out appliqués from nonfloral fabric)

CUTTING

From the large-scale black-and-white floral, cut:
1 square, 14½" x 14½"

From the black-and-white striped fabric, cut:
4 strips, 2½" x 14½"
4 strips, 1½" x 27"

From the pink-and-black print, cut:
4 squares, 2½" x 2½"
4 strips, 4½" x 29"

From the small-scale black-and-white floral, cut:
2 squares, 13⅝" x 13⅝"; cut each square once diagonally to yield 4 triangles
4 squares, 1½" x 1½"
4 squares, 4½" x 4½"

From the black-and-white print for binding, cut:
4 strips, 2⅛" x 42"

Designed and sewn by Debby Kratovil; quilted by Peggy Barkle.

MAKING THE BLOCK

1. Sew a black-and-white striped 2½" x 14½" strip to opposite sides of the large-scale floral square. Press the seam allowances toward the strips. Add a pink-and-black square to the ends of the remaining two striped 2½" x 14½" strips. Press the seam allowances toward the strips. Sew these strips to the remaining two sides of the square.

2. Sew a small-scale floral triangle to each side of the square, joining opposite sides first. Press the seam allowances toward the triangles. The block should measure 26" x 26".

ASSEMBLING THE QUILT TOP

1. Measure the quilt top through the center from side to side and trim two striped 1½" x 27" strips to this measurement. Measure the quilt top from top to bottom and cut the remaining two striped strips to this measurement. Refer to the quilt-assembly diagram to sew the top and bottom strips to the top and bottom edges of the quilt top. Press the seam allowances toward the borders. Add a small-scale floral 1½" square to the ends of each of the remaining two strips, and then sew the strips to the sides of the quilt top. Press the seam allowances toward the borders.

2. Prepare the appliqués. If you are using a floral fabric, follow the manufacturer's instructions to adhere the fusible web to the wrong side of the fabric and cut out eight motifs. Remove the fusible-web paper from the wrong side of each appliqué.

   If you are using the template to make the appliqués, adhere the web to the wrong side of the fabric. *Do not remove the paper.* Trace the pattern at right onto freezer paper and cut it out. Iron the template to the right side of the fused fabric and cut out the shape. Remove the freezer-paper template and the fusible-web paper and repeat the process to make eight appliqués.

3. Arrange the appliqués on the quilt top as desired, referring to the quilt photo as needed. Follow the manufacturer's instructions to fuse the appliqués in place. Stitch around the edge of each appliqué using matching thread and a narrow zigzag stitch.

4 Repeat step 1 with the pink-and-black strips and the small-scale floral 4½" squares to add the outer borders.

Quilt assembly

FINISHING THE QUILT

1 Prepare a backing that is 6" longer and wider than the quilt top.

2 Layer the backing, batting, and quilt top. Pin, hand baste, or spray baste the layers together.

3 Quilt using your preferred method. Trim the excess batting and backing even with the edges of the quilt top.

4 Using the black-and-white 2⅛"-wide strips, make and attach the binding, referring to page 10 as needed.

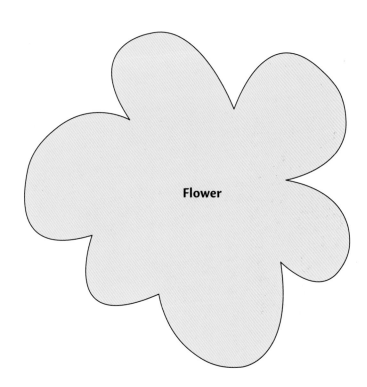

Flower

PATTERN DOES NOT INCLUDE
SEAM ALLOWANCE.

Starry, Starry BRIGHTS

Glorious flowers team up with stars for supersized bouquets of blooms that sparkle even in the night. Large patches capture the vibrant colors, and quick piecing will make this quilt go together in no time!

Block Finished Size: 30" x 30" ■ Number of Blocks in Quilt: 4 ■ Quilt Finished Size: 80" x 80"

MATERIALS

Yardages are based on 42"-wide fabrics.

2⅝ yards of pink-and-orange dot print for outer border and binding

1½ yards of white dot print for blocks

⅞ yard of large-scale multicolored floral for blocks

⅞ yard of purple floral for blocks

⅔ yard of medium lavender print for blocks

⅔ yard of orange print for blocks

⅝ yard of pink-and-orange striped fabric for inner border

⅜ yard of purple striped fabric for blocks

⅜ yard of yellow dot print for blocks

5 yards of fabric for backing

88" x 88" square of batting

CUTTING

From the medium lavender print, cut:

6 strips, 3½" x 42"; crosscut into 64 squares, 3½" x 3½"

From the orange print, cut:

3 strips, 6½" x 42"; crosscut into 16 squares, 6½" x 6½"

From each of the purple striped fabric and yellow dot print, cut:

3 strips, 3½" x 42"; crosscut into 16 rectangles, 3½" x 6½"

From the white dot print, cut:

3 strips, 6½" x 42"; crosscut into 16 squares, 6½" x 6½"

4 strips, 6⅞" x 42"; crosscut into 16 squares, 6⅞" x 6⅞"

From the purple floral, cut:

4 strips, 6⅞" x 42"; crosscut into 16 squares, 6⅞" x 6⅞"

From the large-scale multicolored floral, cut:

4 strips, 6½" x 42"; crosscut into 20 squares, 6½" x 6½"

From the pink-and-orange striped fabric, cut:

7 strips, 2½" x 42"

From the pink-and-orange dot print, cut:

2 strips, 2⅛" x 42"

From the *lengthwise grain* of the remaining pink-and-orange dot print, cut:

4 strips, 8½" x 82"

3 strips, 2⅛" x length of fabric

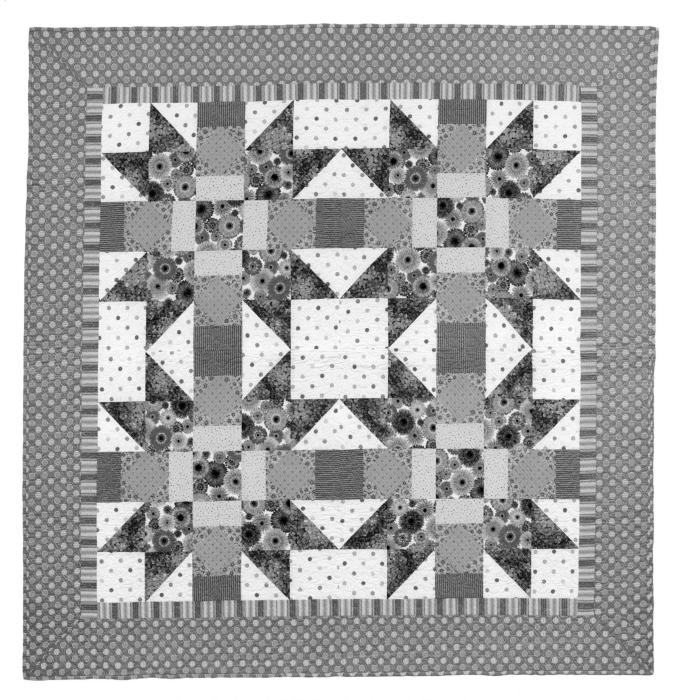

Designed and sewn by Debby Kratovil; machine quilted by Carol Jaynes.

MAKING THE BLOCKS

1 Draw a diagonal line from corner to corner on the wrong side of each lavender square. Position a marked square on opposite corners of an orange square as shown. Sew on the marked lines. Trim ¼" from the lines. Press the resulting triangles outward. Repeat on the remaining two corners of the orange square. Repeat to make a total of 16 square-in-a-square units measuring 6½" square.

Make 16.

2 Sew a purple striped rectangle to one side of each square-in-a-square unit and a yellow rectangle to the opposite side. Make a total of 16 units.

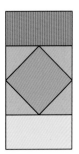

Make 16.

3 Draw a diagonal line from corner to corner on the wrong side of each white 6⅞" square. Place each marked square on top of a purple floral 6⅞" square, right sides together. Secure with a pin. Sew ¼" from each side of the drawn lines. Cut the units apart on the marked lines. Press the units open. Make a total of 32 half-square-triangle units measuring 6½" square.

Make 32.

4 Arrange two half-square-triangle units, one white 6½" square, and one multicolored floral 6½"square into two rows as shown. Sew the pieces in each row together. Press the seam allowances toward the white and multicolored floral squares. Sew the rows together to complete a corner unit. Press the seam allowances open. Repeat to make a total of 16 corner units measuring 12½" square.

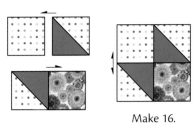

Make 16.

5 Arrange four corner units, four units from step 2, and one multicolored floral square into three rows as shown. Sew the units in each row together. Press the seam allowances open. Sew the rows together. Press the seam allowances open. Repeat to make a total of four blocks measuring 30½" square.

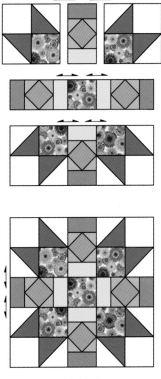

Make 4.

ASSEMBLING THE QUILT TOP

1. Refer to the quilt assembly diagram to arrange the blocks into two rows of two blocks each. Sew the blocks in each row together. Press the seam allowances open. Sew the rows together. Press the seam allowance open. The quilt top should measure 60½" square.

2. Sew the pink-and-orange striped strips together to make one long strip. Press the seam allowances in one direction. Measure the quilt top through the center from side to side. From the pieced strip, cut two strips to this measurement and sew them to the top and bottom edges of the quilt top. Press the seam allowances toward the borders. Measure the quilt top through the center from top to bottom, including the borders. From the remainder of the pieced strip, cut two strips to this measurement and sew them to the sides of the quilt top. Press the seam allowances toward the borders. The quilt top should now measure 64½" square.

3. Refer to "Magical Mitered Corners" on page 10 to add the pink-and-orange dot 8½"-wide border strips to the quilt top.

FINISHING THE QUILT

1. Prepare a backing that is 6" longer and wider than the quilt top.

2. Layer the backing, batting, and quilt top. Pin, hand baste, or spray baste the layers together.

3. Quilt using your preferred method. Trim the excess batting and backing even with the edges of the quilt top.

4. Using the pink-and-orange dot 2⅛"-wide strips, make and attach the binding, referring to page 10 as needed.

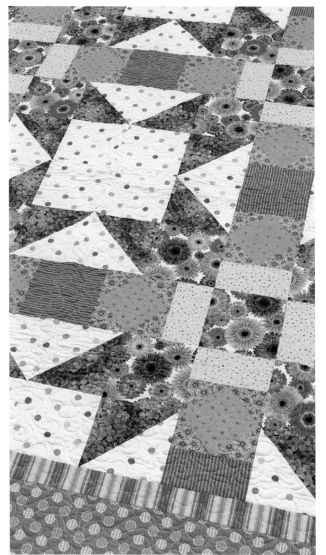

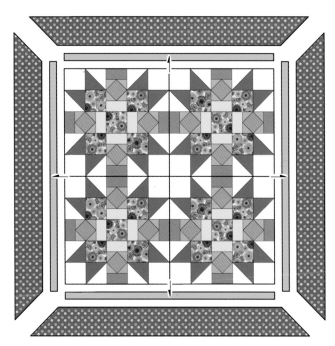

Quilt assembly

TRICK-OR-TREAT *Mice*

Just one block is all it takes to make this quilt. Add some scrappy borders and you have a fun quilt for just about any celebration. This one was created with a Halloween theme, but any holiday, specialty, or novelty fabric will do for an eye-catching focal point that will bring a smile to children of all ages. This is a perfect project for those themed fat-quarter bundles that we find so irresistible!

Block Finished Size: 30" x 30" ■ Number of Blocks in Quilt: 1 ■ Quilt Finished Size: 42½" x 42½"

MATERIALS

Yardages are based on 42"-wide fabrics.

¼ yard of orange print 1 for inner border

1 fat quarter of purple novelty print 1 for block center square and border

1 fat quarter *each* of purple novelty prints 2 and 3 for block and border

1 fat quarter of purple mottled print or solid for block

1 fat quarter of black novelty print 1 for border

1 fat quarter of black novelty print 2 for block

1 fat quarter of green mottled print or solid for block

1 fat quarter of green novelty print for border

1 fat quarter of orange novelty print for block and border

1 fat quarter of orange print 2 for block

1 fat quarter of light yellow print for block

½ yard of black solid for binding

2 yards of fabric for backing

48" x 48" square of batting

CUTTING

After cutting the pieces below, set aside the leftover fabrics for the pieced border.

From the green mottled print or solid, cut:
2 rectangles, 3½" x 6½"
8 squares, 3½" x 3½"
4 squares, 6⅞" x 6⅞"

From the purple novelty print 3, cut:
2 squares, 6½" x 6½"

From the purple mottled print or solid, cut:
2 rectangles, 3½" x 6½"
8 squares, 3½" x 3½"

From the orange novelty print, cut:
2 squares, 6½" x 6½"

From the light yellow print, cut:
4 rectangles, 3½" x 6½"

From the purple novelty print 2, cut:
4 squares, 6⅞" x 6⅞"

From the black novelty print 2, cut:
4 squares, 6½" x 6½"

Designed and sewn by Debby Kratovil; machine quilted by Peggy Barkle.

From the orange print 2, cut:
4 squares, 6½" x 6½"

From the purple novelty print 1, cut:
1 square, 6½" x 6½"

From the orange print 1, cut:
4 strips, 1¼" x 42"

From the black solid, cut:
5 strips, 2⅛" x 42"

MAKING THE BLOCK

1. Draw a diagonal line from corner to corner on the wrong side of each 3½" green square. Position a marked square on opposite corners of a purple novelty print 3 square. Sew on the marked lines. Trim ¼" from the lines. Press the resulting triangles outward. Repeat on the remaining two corners of the purple square. Repeat to make one more purple square-in-a-square unit measuring 6½".

Make 2.

2. Repeat step 1 with the purple mottled squares and the orange novelty squares to make two orange square-in-a-square units.

Make 2.

3. Sew a purple mottled rectangle to one side of each purple square-in-a-square unit and a yellow rectangle to the opposite sides. Press the seam allowances toward the rectangles. Repeat to make a

total of two units. In the same manner, sew a yellow and a green rectangle to opposite ends of each orange square-in-a-square unit.

Make 2 of each.

4. Draw a diagonal line from corner to corner on the wrong side of each 6⅞" green square. Place each marked square on top of a 6⅞" purple novelty print 2 square, right sides together. Secure with a pin. Sew ¼" from each side of the drawn lines. Cut the units apart on the marked lines. Press the units open. Make a total of eight half-square-triangle units measuring 6½" square.

Make 8

5. Arrange two half-square-triangle units, one black novelty print 2 square, and one orange print 2 square into two rows as shown. Sew the pieces in each row together. Press the seam allowances toward the black and orange squares. Sew the rows together to complete a corner unit. Press the seam allowances open. Repeat to make a total of four corner units measuring 12½" square.

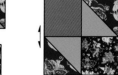

Make 4.

6 Arrange the four corner units, the four units from step 3, and the purple novelty 1 square into three rows as shown. Sew the units in each row together. Press the seam allowances open. Sew the rows together. Press the seam allowances open. The block should measure 30½" square.

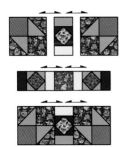
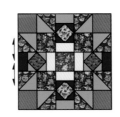

Make 1.

ASSEMBLING THE QUILT TOP

1 Measure the block through the center from top to bottom. Trim two of the orange print 1 strips to this measurement and sew them to the sides of the block. Press the seam allowances toward the borders. Measure the block through the center from side to side, including the borders, and trim the remaining two orange print 1 strips to this measurement. Sew the strips to the top and bottom edges of the block. The quilt top should measure 32" square.

2 From the leftover novelty-print fat quarters and the black novelty print 1 and green novelty print fat quarters, cut 6"-wide pieces in various lengths from 4" to 8". If you are using a directional print, cut some pieces from the lengthwise *and* crosswise directions if possible so you can use them for the side borders as well as the top and bottom borders. You will add the top border first, and then work clockwise around the quilt to add the remaining border strips. Plan accordingly. Randomly join several pieces to make a strip 32" long, trimming the strip as necessary. Refer to the quilt-assembly diagram to sew the border to the top edge of the

quilt top. Press the seam allowance toward the border. Randomly join several more pieces to make two strips 37½" long, trimming as necessary. Sew these strips to the right-hand side and then the bottom edge of the quilt top. Press the seam allowances toward the borders. Join and trim the remaining pieces to make a strip 43" long. Sew this strip to the left-hand side of the quilt top. Press the seam allowance toward the border.

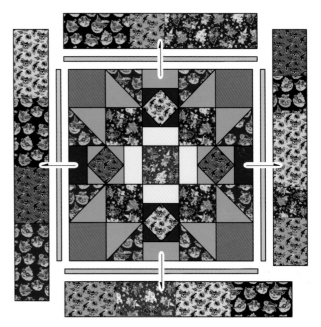

Quilt assembly

FINISHING THE QUILT

1 Prepare a backing that is 6" longer and wider than the quilt top.

2 Layer the backing, batting, and quilt top. Pin, hand baste, or spray baste the layers together.

3 Quilt using your preferred method. Trim the excess batting and backing even with the edges of the quilt top.

4 Using the 2⅛"-wide black strips, make and attach the binding, referring to page 10 as needed.

DIADEM

Don't be fooled by the holiday fabric. This quilt is perfect for any large-scale print that you love but would hate to cut into small pieces. Showcase large pieces of your favorite floral or geometric fabric, letting it take center stage in this dynamic and easy quilt. The block's four corners are paper pieced for very, very sharp points.

Block Finished Size: 14" x 14" ■ Number of Blocks in Quilt: 4 ■ Quilt Finished Size: 53" x 53"

MATERIALS

Yardages are based on 42"-wide fabrics.

1¾ yards of large-scale dark floral for border and binding

1⅛ yards of large-scale light floral for blocks and sashing strips

⅝ yard of red-and-black striped fabric for sashing strips

½ yard of light print for block backgrounds

⅜ yard of green print for blocks and sashing squares

¼ yard of red print for blocks

3½ yards of fabric for backing

60" x 60" square of batting

Foundation paper

Freezer paper

CUTTING

From the light print, cut:
4 strips, 3" x 42"

From the red print, cut:
1 strip, 6" x 42"; crosscut into 8 rectangles, 4" x 6"

From the green print, cut:
1 strip, 6" x 42"; crosscut into 8 rectangles, 4" x 6"

1 strip, 4½" x 42"; crosscut into 9 squares, 4½" x 4½"

From the large-scale light floral, cut:
4 squares, 10⅜" x 10⅜"

6 strips, 2½" x 42"; crosscut into 12 strips, 2½" x 14½"

From the red-and-black striped fabric, cut:
12 strips, 1½" x 42"; crosscut into 24 strips, 1½" x 14½"

From the *lengthwise grain* of the large-scale dark floral, cut:
2 strips, 7" x 42"

2 strips, 7" x 56"

4 strips, 2⅛" x length of fabric

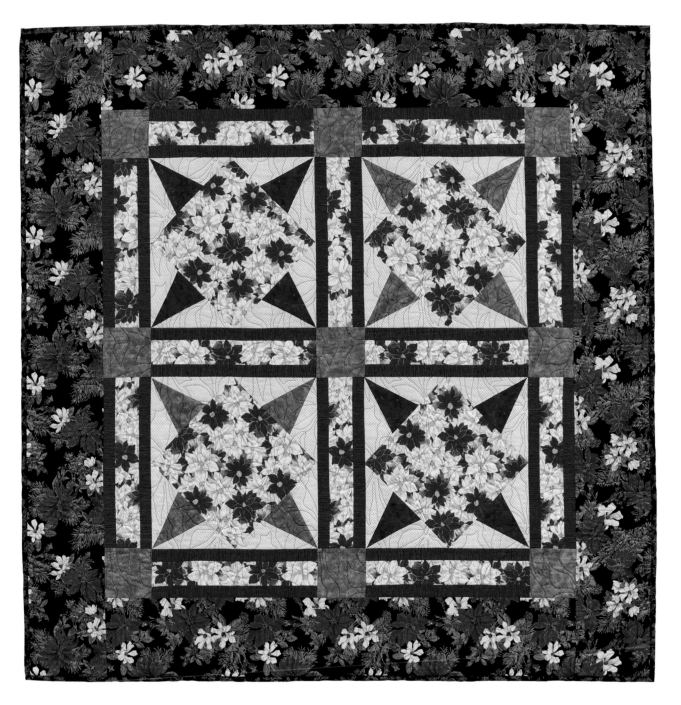

Designed and sewn by Debby Kratovil; machine quilted by Cathy MacDonald.

MAKING THE BLOCKS

1. Trace the pattern on page 97 onto freezer paper and cut it out. This will be the pattern for cutting the pieces for areas 2 and 3 of the paper-pieced corners. Using the template will give you pieces with the correct angle and prevent you from wasting fabric, or worse, sewing pieces that are too short and having to rip them out.

2. Fold a light 3" x 42" strip in half crosswise, wrong sides together. Iron the freezer-paper template to the right side of the strip and cut out the pieces. Rotate the template as shown and iron it to the strip again. Cut out the pieces. Repeat two more times to cut a total of eight pieces from the strip. Half of the pieces will be mirror images of each other. Repeat with the remaining light 3" x 42" strips to cut a total of 32 pieces.

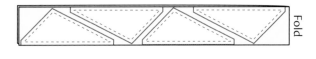

Fold

Area 2 piece.
Cut 16.

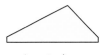

Area 3 piece.
Cut 16.

3. Refer to "Paper Piecing" on page 7 to make 16 copies of the block corner pattern on page 96 using your preferred method. Paper piece each unit, using the red and green rectangles for area 1 and the light pieces you cut in step 2 for areas 2 and 3. Make eight corner units with red points and eight corner units with green points.

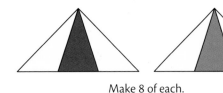

Make 8 of each.

4. Sew four matching corner units to the sides of each light floral square, sewing opposite sides first. Press the seam allowances toward the square. The blocks should measure 14½" square.

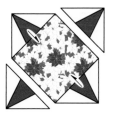

Make 2.

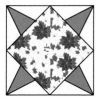

Make 2.

ASSEMBLING THE QUILT TOP

1. Sew a red-and-black striped strip to both long edges of each light floral strip. Press the seam allowances toward the red-and-black strips. Repeat to make a total of 12 sashing strips.

Make 12.

2. Alternately join three green squares and two sashing strips to make a sashing row. Press the seam allowances toward the strips. Repeat to make a total of three sashing rows.

Make 3.

3 Alternately join three sashing strips, one red block, and one green block to make a block row. Press the seam allowances toward the strips. Repeat to make a total of two rows.

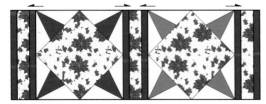

Make 2.

4 Refer to the quilt assembly diagram to alternately sew the sashing rows and block rows together. Press the seam allowances toward the sashing rows. The quilt top should measure 40½" square.

5 Measure the quilt top through the center from side to side. Trim the dark floral 7" x 42" strips to this measurement and sew them to the top and bottom edges of the quilt top. Press the seam allowances toward the borders. Measure the quilt top through the center from top to bottom, including the borders. Trim the dark floral 7" x 56" strips to this measurement and sew them to the sides of the quilt top. Press the seam allowances toward the borders.

FINISHING THE QUILT

1 Prepare a backing that is 6" longer and wider than the quilt top.

2 Layer the backing, batting, and quilt top. Pin, hand baste, or spray baste the layers together.

3 Quilt using your preferred method. Trim the excess batting and backing even with the edges of the quilt top.

4 Using the dark floral 2⅛"-wide strips, make and attach the binding, referring to page 10 as needed.

Quilt assembly

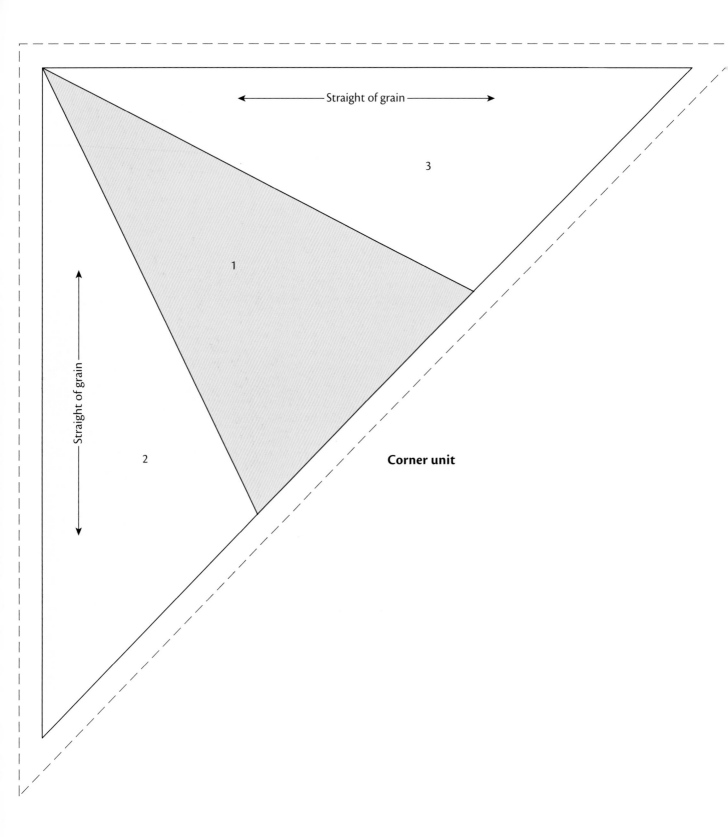

Straight of grain

3

1

Straight of grain

2

Corner unit

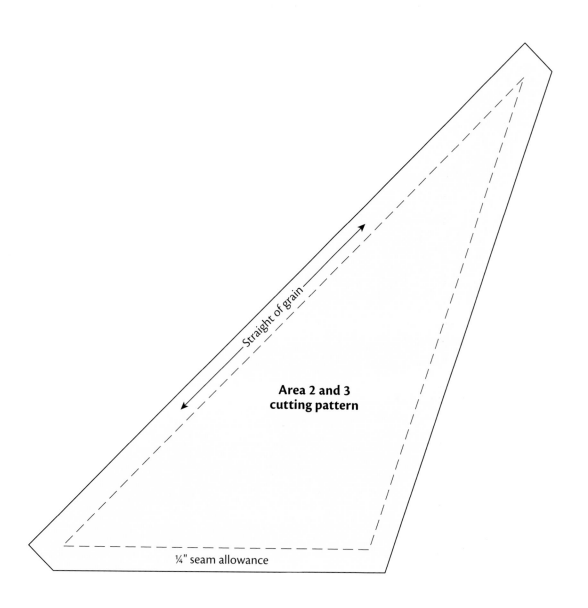

Straight of grain

**Area 2 and 3
cutting pattern**

¼" seam allowance

CARRIAGE *Crossing*

This quilt combines two similar blocks: Railroad Crossing and At the Depot. The nine 15" blocks are arranged so that the red fabric makes a bold, diagonal statement. The fabrics lend an aged and comfortable feeling to the quilt.

Block Finished Size: 15¼" x 15¼" ■ Number of Blocks in Quilt: 9 ■ Quilt Finished Size: 77¾" x 77¾"

MATERIALS

Yardages are based on 42"-wide fabrics.

2½ yards of large-scale floral for outer border and At the Depot blocks

2 yards of tan print for block backgrounds and first and third borders

1½ yards of blue print 1 for blocks, second border, and binding

1¼ yards of green print for Railroad Crossing blocks and second border

⅞ yard of red print 1 for Railroad Crossing blocks and second border

⅞ yard of red print 2 for Railroad Crossing blocks and second border

½ yard of blue print 2 for At the Depot blocks

¼ yard of blue print 3 for At the Depot blocks

7 yards of fabric for backing

85" x 85" square of batting

Spray starch or sizing

CUTTING

From the green print, cut:

8 strips, 2¼" x 42"

8 strips, 2½" x 42"

From the red print 2, cut:

4 strips, 2¼" x 42"

4 strips, 2½" x 42"

2 squares, 6⅞" x 6⅞"; cut each square once diagonally to yield 4 half-square triangles

From the tan print, cut:

3 strips, 9½" x 42"; crosscut into 9 squares, 9½" x 9½". Cut each square twice diagonally to yield 36 quarter-square triangles.

5 strips, 3" x 42"

7 strips, 2½" x 42"

From the red print 1, cut:

2 strips, 5" x 42"; crosscut into 10 squares, 5" x 5". Cut each square once diagonally to yield 20 half-square triangles.

6 strips, 2½" x 42"

Designed, sewn, and quilted by Abigail Dolinger.

From the **blue print 1 fabric**, cut:

1 strip, 7½" x 42"

6 strips, 2½" x 42"

1 strip, 5¾" x 42"; crosscut into 5 squares, 5¾" x 5¾"

9 strips, 2⅛" x 42"

From the **blue print 2 fabric**, cut:

3 strips, 2½" x 42"

1 strip, 5" x 42"; crosscut into 8 squares, 5" x 5". Cut each square once diagonally to yield 16 half-square triangles.

From the **blue print 3 fabric**, cut:

3 strips, 2½" x 42"

From the *lengthwise grain* of the **large-scale floral print**, cut:

4 strips, 6" x 80"

From the remainder of the **large-scale floral print**, fussy cut:

4 squares, 5¾" x 5¾", centering a floral motif

MAKING THE RAILROAD CROSSING BLOCKS

1 Sew a 2¼" x 42" green strip to both long edges of a 2¼" x 42" red print 2 strip to make a strip set measuring 5¾" wide. Press the seam allowances toward the green strips. Repeat to make a total of four strip sets. Crosscut the strip sets into 20 segments, 6" wide.

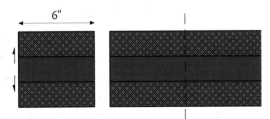

Make 4 strip sets.
Cut 20 segments.

2 Sew the short edges of two tan triangles to the 6" sides of a step 1 segment, aligning the lower edges. The triangles are cut oversized and will be trimmed later. Press the seam allowances toward the triangles. Center the long edge of a red print 1 triangle along the top edge of the segment and sew it in place. Press the seam allowance toward

the triangle. Trim the sides ¼" from the upper points of the step 1 segment. Repeat to make a total of 10 corner units.

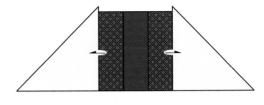

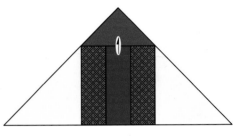

Make 10.

3 Sew a blue print 1 square between two segments from step 1. Press the seam allowances toward the square. Center and sew a red print 1 triangle to the ends of the strip. Again, the triangles are cut oversized and will be trimmed later. Press the seam allowances toward the segments. Repeat to make a total of five center units.

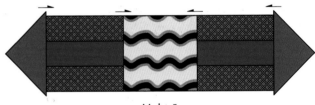

Make 5.

4 Arrange two corner units and one center unit as shown. Sew the units together, matching seam allowances. Press the seam allowances toward the center unit. Trim the excess red triangles of the center section even with the edges of the corner sections. Repeat to make a total of five Railroad Crossing blocks measuring 15¾" square.

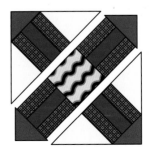

Railroad Crossing block.
Make 5.

MAKING THE AT THE DEPOT BLOCKS

1 Using the 2½" x 42" strips, sew one blue print 2 and one blue print 3 strip to the long edges of a blue print 1 strip to make a strip set measuring 6" wide. Press the seam allowances toward the blue print 2 and 3 strips. Repeat to make a total of three strip sets. Crosscut the strip sets into 16 segments, 5¾" wide.

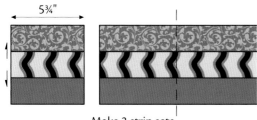

5¾"

Make 3 strip sets.
Cut 16 segments.

2 Sew the short edges of two tan triangles to the 6" sides of a step 1 segment, aligning the lower edges. The triangles are cut oversize and will be trimmed later. Press the seam allowances toward the triangles. Center the long edge of a blue print 2 triangle along the top edge of the segment and sew it in place. Press the seam allowance toward the triangle. Trim the sides ¼" from the upper points of the step 1 segment. Repeat to make a total of eight corner units.

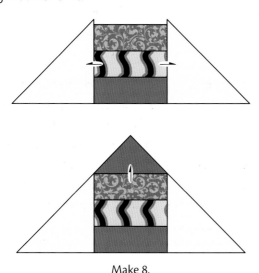

Make 8.

3 Sew a floral square between two segments from step 1. Press the seam allowances toward the square. Center and sew a blue print 2 triangle to the ends of the strip. Again, the triangles are cut oversize and will be trimmed later. Press the seam allowances toward the segments. Repeat to make a total of four center units.

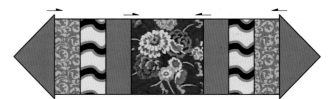

Make 4.

4 Arrange two corner units and one center unit as shown. Sew the units together. Press the seam allowances toward the center unit. Trim the excess blue triangles of the center section even with the edges of the corner sections. Repeat to make a total of four At the Depot blocks measuring 15¾" square.

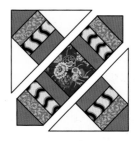

At the Depot block.
Make 4.

ASSEMBLING THE PIECED BORDER UNITS

1 Sew a 2½" x 42" green strip to both long edges of a 2½" x 42" red print 2 strip to make a strip set measuring 6½" wide. Press the seam allowances toward the green strips. Repeat to make a total of four strip sets. Crosscut the strip sets into 16 segments, 7¾" wide.

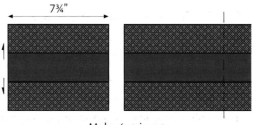

7¾"

Make 4 strip sets.
Cut 16 segments.

2 Sew a 2½" x 42" red print 1 strip to both long edges of a 2½" x 42" blue print 1 strip to make a strip set measuring 6½" wide. Press the seam allowances toward the blue strip. Repeat to make a total of three strip sets. Crosscut the strip sets into 12 segments, 7¾" wide.

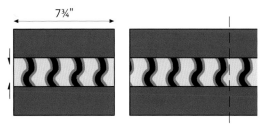

7¾"

Make 3 strip sets.
Cut 12 segments.

3 Apply spray starch to the 7½" x 42" blue print 1 strip. This will help avoid stretching the bias pieces that you'll cut. Fold the strip in half crosswise and straighten the edge if needed. Using a ruler that is at least 7" square, place the ruler diagonally along the straightened edge so that the 6⅞" mark on two adjacent sides of the ruler are aligned with the edge. Cut along the two edges to make two triangles. Repeat to cut a total of four triangles.

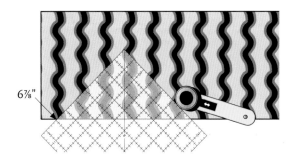

6⅞"

4 Sew each blue print 1 triangle to a red print 2 triangle to make a half-square-triangle unit.

Make 4.

ASSEMBLING THE QUILT TOP

1 Refer to the quilt assembly diagram to arrange the blocks into three rows of three blocks each, alternating the blocks within each row and from row to row. Sew the blocks in each row together. Press the seam allowances open. The quilt center should measure 46¼" square.

2 Sew the 3" x 42" tan strips together end to end to make one long piece. From the pieced strip, cut two strips 46¼" and sew them to the top and bottom edges of the quilt top. Press the seam allowances toward the borders. From the remainder of the pieced strip, cut two strips 51¼". Sew the strips to the sides of the quilt top. Press the seam allowances toward the borders. The quilt top should measure 51¼" square. It is important that this measurement is correct in order for the pieced second border to fit.

3 Alternately join four green-and-red segments and three red-and-blue segments from steps 1 and 2 of "Assembling the Pieced Border Units." Press the seam allowances open. Repeat to make a total of four pieced border strips.

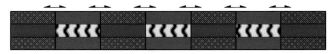

Make 4.

4 Refer to the quilt assembly diagram to sew a pieced border strip to the top and bottom edges of the quilt top. Press the seam allowances toward the first border. Add a half-square-triangle unit from step 4 of "Assembling the Pieced Border Units" to the ends of the remaining border strips. Be careful that the blue triangles are positioned correctly. Sew these borders to the sides of the quilt top. Press the seam allowances toward the first border.

5 Sew the 2½" x 42" tan strips together end to end to make one long strip. Measure the quilt top through the center from side to side. From the pieced strip, cut two strips to this measurement and sew them to the top and bottom edges of the quilt top. Press the seam allowances toward the newly added border. Measure the quilt top through the center from top to bottom, including the borders. From the remainder of the pieced strip, cut two strips to this measurement and sew them to the sides of the quilt top.

6 Refer to "Magical Mitered Corners" on page 10 to add the 6"-wide floral border strips to the quilt top.

FINISHING THE QUILT

1 Prepare a backing that is 6" longer and wider than the quilt top.

2 Layer the backing, batting, and quilt top. Pin, hand baste, or spray baste the layers together.

3 Quilt using your preferred method. Trim the excess batting and backing even with the edges of the quilt top.

4 Using the 2⅛"-wide blue print 1 strips, make and attach the binding, referring to page 10 as needed.

Quilt assembly

Cloisonné DIAMONDS

I have a lot of diamonds and they're all made of cloth! This quilt features 60° floral diamonds alternating with two-color four-patch diamonds. Dots, circles, stripes, and flowers create a stunning garden of year-round color. Even though these blocks aren't oversized, the print is large scale.

Block Finished Size: 7" x 12" ■ Number of Blocks in Quilt: 59 ■ Quilt Finished Size: 70" x 81"

MATERIALS

Yardages are based on 42"-wide fabrics.

2⅝ yards of multicolored striped fabric for outer border and binding

1½ yards of large-scale multicolored floral for Diamond blocks

⅞ yard of light print for setting triangles

⅔ yard of blue solid for Four Patch Diamond blocks

⅔ yard of medium brown solid for Four Patch Diamond blocks

⅔ yard of blue print for first border

½ yard of magenta print for second border

5 yards of fabric for backing

78" x 89" piece of batting

CUTTING

From the large-scale multicolored floral, cut:
7 strips, 6½" x 42"

From the blue solid, cut:
6 strips, 3½" x 42"

From the medium brown solid, cut:
6 strips, 3½" x 42"

From the light print, cut:
4 strips, 6¾" x 42". From 2 strips, cut 12 triangles using pattern A (page 108). Fold the remaining 2 strips in half lengthwise, right sides together, and cut 10 pairs of half triangles using pattern B/Br (page 109).

From the blue print, cut:
6 strips, 3½" x 42"

From the magenta print, cut:
6 strips, 1½" x 42"

From the *lengthwise grain* of the multicolored striped fabric, cut:
2 strips, 7" x 83"
2 strips, 7" x 72"
4 strips, 2⅛" x length of fabric

Designed and sewn by Debby Kratovil; machine quilted by Peggy Barkle.

MAKING THE BLOCKS

1 Trim one end of each floral strip at a 60° angle. Place the angled end so it is on the left. Measure 6½" from the angled end and make another cut to create a Diamond block. Repeat to cut a total of 35 Diamond blocks. You should be able to cut five diamonds from each strip.

Cut 35 Diamond blocks.

2 Stitch a blue solid strip to a brown strip along the long edges, offsetting the strips 2", to make a strip set. Press the seam allowance toward the blue strip. Repeat to make a total of six strip sets. Trim one end of each strip at a 60° angle. Place the angled end so it is on the left. Measure 3½" from the angled end and make another cut. Repeat to cut a total of 48 segments.

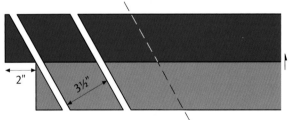

Make 6 strip sets.
Cut 48 segments.

3 Sew two segments together as shown to make a Four Patch Diamond block.

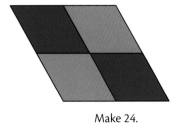

Make 24.

ASSEMBLING THE QUILT TOP

1 Sew one template B triangle and one template B reversed triangle together along the short edges. Repeat to make a total of eight side setting triangles. The remaining four half-triangle shapes are for the four corners.

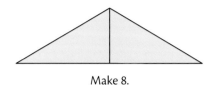

Make 8.

2 Refer to the quilt assembly diagram to arrange the Diamond blocks, the Four Patch Diamond blocks, the side setting triangles, the 12 light template A triangles, and the remaining template B and B reversed half triangles into diagonal rows as shown. Join the pieces in each row. You will be working with bias edges, so take care to not stretch the fabric. Press the seam allowances toward the Diamond blocks in each row. This will make for easier joining of the rows because the seams will nestle snugly against each other. Join the rows, adding the four corner triangles last. Press the seam allowances away from the center row.

3 Sew the blue print strips together end to end to make one long strip. Measure the quilt top through the center from side to side. From the pieced strip, cut two strips to this measurement and sew them to the top and bottom edges of the quilt top. Press the seam allowances toward the borders. Measure the quilt top through the center from top to bottom, including the borders. From the remainder of the pieced strip, cut two strips to this measurement. Sew the strips to the sides of the quilt top. Press the seam allowances toward the borders.

4 Repeat step 3 with the magenta strips to add the second border to the quilt top.

5 Refer to "Magical Mitered Corners" on page 10 to add the multicolored striped 7"-wide strips to the quilt top, using the longer strips for the sides of the quilt.

FINISHING THE QUILT

1 Prepare a backing that is 6" longer and wider than the quilt top.

2 Layer the backing, batting, and quilt top. Pin, hand baste, or spray baste the layers together.

3 Quilt using your preferred method. Trim the excess batting and backing even with the edges of the quilt top.

4 Using the multicolored striped $2\frac{1}{8}$"-wide strips, make and attach the binding, referring to page 10 as needed.

Quilt assembly

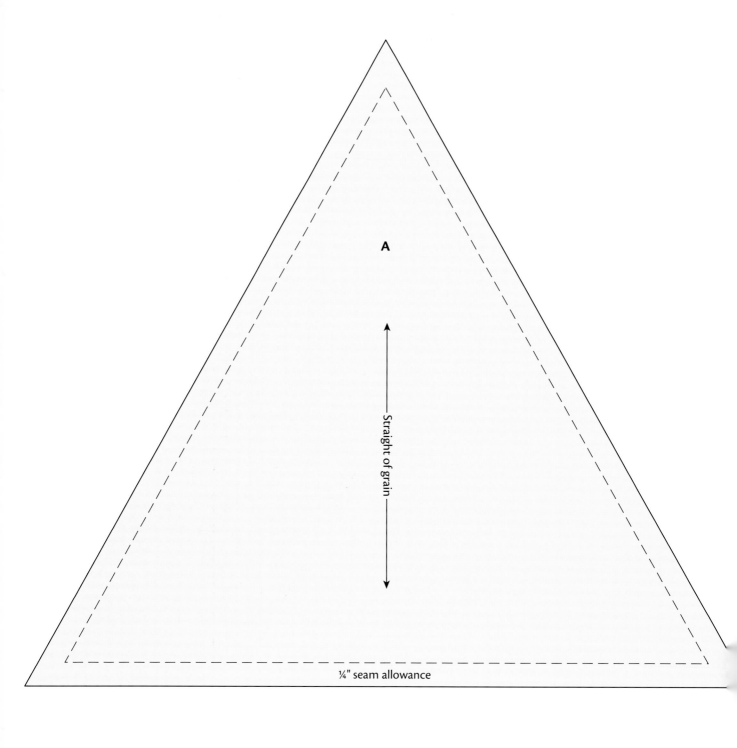

A

Straight of grain

¼" seam allowance

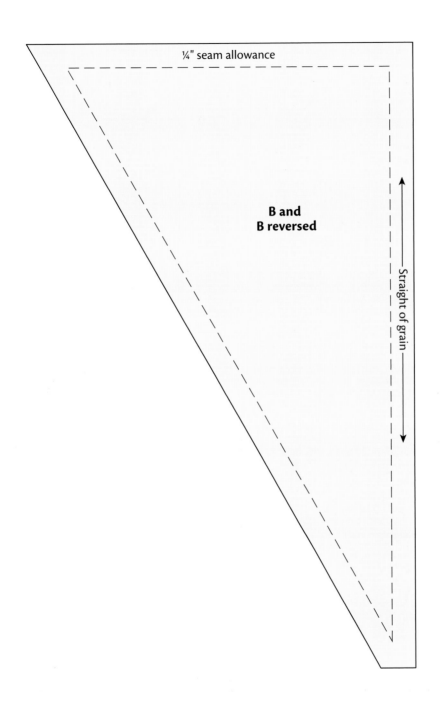

¼" seam allowance

**B and
B reversed**

Straight of grain

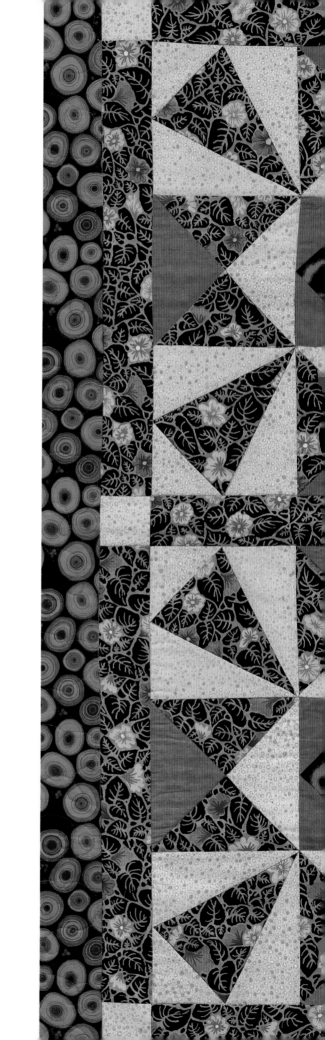

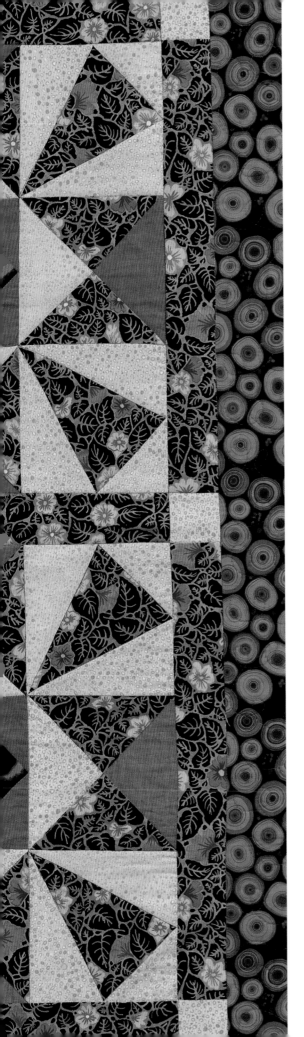

ABOUT THE *Author*

Debby Kratovil has been "sewing for the camera" for more than 15 years. She has been a major contributor to several quilting publications during that time, with more than 600 articles published. She says she is a regular cover girl, with at least 25 of her quilts making the cover of quilting magazines. She makes samples and project sheets for several fabric companies and revels in all that luscious fabric. She is the author of the *Quilter's Block-a-Day Calendar* and companion CD (Martingale & Company, 2007). Debby likes to say, "I've never met a fabric I didn't like." One of her special talents is making a beautiful quilt using challenging fabric collections. She is on very good terms with her computer and computerized sewing machines, so she can take a project from start to finish quickly. She's always planning her next design and starts with "what if?" and gets going with "why not?" Debby is a prolific quilter, designer, and illustrator. Best of all, she enjoys every minute of it.

She is a popular teacher, both locally and nationally, as many happy students will attest. She loves being in the classroom with motivated quilting students. Her patterns are clear, well illustrated, and simple so that even the beginner can tackle a project with confidence.

Her website, www.quilterbydesign.com, is one of the oldest quilting websites on the Internet. She lives in Bristow, Virginia, with her husband, Phil, and dog, Belle. She has three grown daughters, none of whom quilt—yet.

NEW AND BESTSELLING TITLES FROM

 That Patchwork Place® America's Best-Loved Quilt Books®

 Martingale® & COMPANY America's Best-Loved Craft & Hobby Books®
America's Best-Loved Knitting Books®

APPLIQUÉ
Applique Quilt Revival
Beautiful Blooms
Cutting-Garden Quilts
Dream Landscapes—*NEW!*
More Fabulous Flowers
Sunbonnet Sue and Scottie Too

BABIES AND CHILDREN
Baby's First Quilts—*NEW!*
Baby Wraps
Even More Quilts for Baby
Let's Pretend—*NEW!*
The Little Box of Baby Quilts
Snuggle-and-Learn Quilts for Kids
Sweet and Simple Baby Quilts

BEGINNER
Color for the Terrified Quilter
Happy Endings, Revised Edition
Machine Appliqué for the Terrified Quilter
Your First Quilt Book (or it should be!)

GENERAL QUILTMAKING
Adventures in Circles
American Jane's Quilts for All Seasons—*NEW!*
Bits and Pieces
Charmed
Cool Girls Quilt
Country-Fresh Quilts—*NEW!*
Creating Your Perfect Quilting Space
Follow-the-Line Quilting Designs Volume Three
Gathered from the Garden
The New Handmade—*NEW!*
Points of View
Positively Postcards
Prairie Children and Their Quilts
Quilt Revival
A Quilter's Diary
Quilter's Happy Hour
Quilting for Joy—*NEW!*
Sensational Sashiko
Simple Seasons
Skinny Quilts and Table Runners

Twice Quilted
Young at Heart Quilts

HOLIDAY AND SEASONAL
Christmas Quilts from Hopscotch
Christmas with Artful Offerings
Comfort and Joy
Holiday Wrappings

HOOKED RUGS, NEEDLE FELTING, AND PUNCHNEEDLE
The Americana Collection
Miniature Punchneedle Embroidery
Needle-Felting Magic
Needle Felting with Cotton and Wool
Punchneedle Fun

PAPER PIECING
Easy Reversible Vests, Revised Edition—*NEW!*
Paper-Pieced Mini Quilts
Show Me How to Paper Piece
Showstopping Quilts to Foundation Piece
A Year of Paper Piecing

PIECING
501 Rotary-Cut Quilt Blocks—*NEW!*
Better by the Dozen
Favorite Traditional Quilts Made Easy—*NEW!*
Loose Change—*NEW!*
Maple Leaf Quilts
Mosaic Picture Quilts
New Cuts for New Quilts
Nine by Nine
On-Point Quilts
Quiltastic Curves
Ribbon Star Quilts
Rolling Along
Sew One and You're Done

QUICK QUILTS
40 Fabulous Quick-Cut Quilts
Instant Bargello
Quilts on the Double
Sew Fun, Sew Colorful Quilts

SCRAP QUILTS
Nickel Quilts
Save the Scraps
Simple Strategies for Scrap Quilts
Spotlight on Scraps

CRAFTS
Art from the Heart
The Beader's Handbook
Card Design
Crochet for Beaders
Dolly Mama Beads
Embellished Memories—*NEW!*
Friendship Bracelets All Grown Up
Making Beautiful Jewelry—*NEW!*
Paper It!—*NEW!*
Sculpted Threads
Sew Sentimental
Trading Card Treasures—*NEW!*

KNITTING & CROCHET
365 Crochet Stitches a Year
365 Knitting Stitches a Year
A to Z of Knitting
All about Knitting—*NEW!*
Amigurumi World
Beyond Wool—*NEW!*
Cable Confidence
Casual, Elegant Knits
Chic Knits
Crocheted Pursenalities
Gigi Knits…and Purls
Kitty Knits
Knitted Finger Puppets—*NEW!*
The Knitter's Book of Finishing Techniques
Knitting Circles around Socks
Knitting with Gigi
More Sensational Knitted Socks
Pursenalities
Skein for Skein
Toe-Up Techniques for Hand Knit Socks, Revised Edition—*NEW!*
Together or Separate—*NEW!*

2 1982 02418 5377

Our books are available at bookstores and your favorite craft, fabric, and yarn retailers. If you don't see the title you're looking for, visit us at **www.martingale-pub.com** or contact us at:

1-800-426-3126

International: 1-425-483-3313
Fax: 1-425-486-7596 • **Email:** info@martingale-pub.com